JUNE WILLSON READ

Frontier Madam

THE LIFE OF DELL BURKE, LADY OF LUSK

TWODOT®

GUILFORD, CONNECTICUT
HELENA, MONTANA
AN IMPRINT OF THE GLOBE PEQUOT PRESS

A · TWODOT® · BOOK

Copyright © 2008 by June Willson Read

TwoDot is a registered trademark of The Globe Pequot Press.

Text design: Lisa Reneson

Library of Congress Cataloging-in-Publication Data is available.
ISBN 978-0-7627-4439-8

Manufactured in the United States of America
First Edition/First Printing

CONTENTS

EVERYBODY LIKES DELL—BUT MOST AVOID HER

Over the years, Dell Burke has helped scores of people down on their luck. She has always been a good touch for any fund drive.

"She's had this place in the palm of her hand for years," confided one civic leader.

"She loaned the town money during the Depression, single-handedly floated a water-sewer-and-light bond issues [*sic*], bailed us out when we were about to go under."

Yet, women will cross the street to purposely avoid her. So do most of the men—some with good reason.

"They all know me," said Dell with a touch of sadness in her husky voice. "But all they do is nod and smile."

Dell Burke has been in business just off Main Street continuously over the past fifty-four years, running the two-story frame, always freshly painted Yellow Hotel.

In the vernacular of the Old West, the Yellow Hotel is now and always has been "a sporting house."

—Excerpt from interview by Charles Hillinger,
The *Los Angeles Times,* March 26, 1973

PREFACE

I grew up on a ranch halfway between Lusk and Manville, Wyoming, and to the best of my knowledge, I never saw Dell Burke or any of her girls. I became intrigued by her when I attended her 1981 estate sale the year after she died. Listening to people tell anecdotes about her made me feel that hers was a story begging to be told in full; however, I was too focused on beginning my psychotherapy career to pursue it then.

When I visited Wyoming about twenty years later, I was excited to discover her mystique and history were still vivid in the memory of many people and began talking with those who had known Dell. I spent countless hours talking with more than a hundred people from across the country in the five years I researched this book; there still are pieces of Dell's life that elude discovery. I wish I could have known her when she was alive, but then I might not have known her as well as I do now that I have had the privilege of learning about both sides of the double life she lived. Dell was a private person who dealt with both her shame and success with dignity and integrity.

Most episodes described in this book came directly from people who knew or had heard of Dell Burke. Some are based on information gathered from interviewees and history about that time period. Conversations in this book are fictitious dialogue based on first-hand accounts by interviewees and historical research and represent what Dell might have said. The events describing Dell's move out of her marriage and into prostitution are based on multiple reports from interviewees and her family, along with history of that period. A similar technique was employed at several other points in her story.

When I began researching this biography in 2000, I had no idea I would be beholden to so many for so much—information, support, ideas, contacts, and financial assistance.

Proper appreciation would require writing an entire chapter to thank everyone, so my generic appreciation to the majority will have to suffice. If your name is not specifically listed, please don't be offended; it does not reflect a lack of appreciation for your help. Special thanks go to:

• The young lady in the Sundance Museum whose intriguing comments indicated that Dell's life story was still alive twenty years after her death.

• Loraine Fisher, whose insights, memories, and boxes of her great-aunt Dell's memorabilia provided a wonderful opportunity to collaborate as we pieced the two sides of the story together, aided by her mother, Phyllis.

• My family, whose loving support, information, and ideas helped make this book possible. Thanks to my siblings, Phyllis, Jim, Mary Jean, and George; my daughter, Peggy; my niece, Chris; my son, Michael; and my life partner, Bill Martin.

• The ladies at the Stage Coach Museum in Lusk, the staffs at the museum in Worland and the Niobrara County Library of Lusk, and Arlene Eklund-Ernst at the Pioneer Memorial Museum in Douglas, all of whom provided information and assistance.

• The more than one hundred people who sat for hours sharing their memories and experiences of Dell, as well as others who came forward with information, newspaper clips, and memorabilia.

- Friends whose guidance and support helped sustain progress over the years—George Wm. Treat Flint, Sharon Logan, Peggy Rooks, and Gene Holm.

- The numerous members of the Writers' Group of the Triad, Greensboro, North Carolina, whose support and guidance through the years has been most meaningful: editing by Mary Ferryman, J. J. Benson, Rebecca Chaney, Al Perry, and Nancy Gates; promotional materials from Bob Webb; business cards by Linda Newsom; genealogical assistance from Bob and Mary Webb; cover art by Connie Usry; and much critiquing by the Nonfiction Group members.

- I am grateful to editors Erin Turner and Stephanie Hester and The Globe Pequot Press for making it possible to share Dell's story with readers.

—June Willson Read, Ph.D.

THE LIFE AND TIMES OF
MARIE FISHER/DELL BURKE

1888	July 5, Mary Ada is born to John and Almeda Fisher, Somerset, Ohio
1890	May 3, Branson Jeremiah "Jerry" is born to Delbert and Melissa Dull, Rockford, Ohio
1898	The Fisher family leaves Ohio for the Dakota Territory
1905	November 12, Marie, age seventeen, marries Stephen Law, age twenty-four
	November 12, Charles Fisher, Marie's brother, marries Nora
1910–1912	Marie leaves Stephen Law and moves to Canada, then to Alaska
1911–1916	Progressive Movement forms to stamp out gambling, alcohol abuse, and prostitution
1914	Marie moves to Butte, Montana, and adopts the name of Dell Burke
1917–1918	Dell moves to the Sandbar in Casper, Wyoming
1918	Wyoming adopts the 18th Amendment, enacting Prohibition

1919	Casper declares "war on vice," causing Dell and Bessie Housley to move to Lusk, Wyoming, where they rent a house and go into business
1920	Dell and Bessie purchase a modest house on Lots 8 & 9, Original Town (OT) of Lusk, on First Street for their first brothel
1921	September 29, Almeda Cotterman Fisher (Dell's mother) dies at age sixty-nine
1922	Charlie, Dell's brother, mysteriously disappears, leaving behind his wife and five children in Montana
1924	November 15, John Fisher (Dell's father) dies at age seventy-four
1927	August, Dell purchases Lot 10, OT of Lusk, adjoining the first brothel, and moves in a larger hotel from Manville; she paints it yellow
1929	Dell reportedly purchases bonds for new equipment for the Lusk Municipal Power Plant
	March 12, following Bessie's death, Dell purchases Bessie's share of first house
1930	March 11, Judge C. O. Brown of Sixth Judicial District Court charges Dell with operating a resort on First Street in Lusk and authorizes an injunction to close the Yellow Hotel for the rest of that year
	July 24, Jerry Dull is injured while unloading oil-well drilling materials

1931	Nora Fisher, Charles's wife, works for Dell
	Roy Traver Fisher, Charlie's son, spends the next summer with Dell and Jerry
1933	March 31, Dell's Pekinese dog, Chen Chen, dies
	The 21st Amendment is enacted, repealing the 18th Amendment and ending Prohibition
1935	April, Wyoming officials legalize the sale of hard liquor and beer
	Dolores, Charlie's youngest daughter, drowns in a Michigan lake
1938	August, Dell purchases lots 2–7 OT of Lusk, east of the Yellow Hotel
1946	Nora, Charlie's wife, dies
1949	Doris, Charlie's daughter, dies after being bitten by a rabid dog
1950	June, Dell purchases lots 11 and 12 OT of Lusk, making her the owner of all but one lot on that block
1955	June 4, Jerry Dull dies of a heart attack at age sixty-five
1969	October 23, Charles's son, Roy Traver, dies
1979	August 4, Dell breaks her hip and is hospitalized
1980	November 4, Dell dies of congestive heart failure and pneumonia at the Lusk Nursing Home at age ninety-two
1981	August 15–16 Dell Burke's estate sale held in Lusk, Wyoming

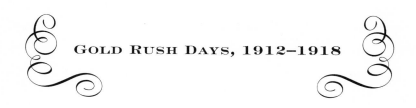

GOLD RUSH DAYS, 1912–1918

The harsh words of the bitter fight with Stephen resounded through Marie's head.

"You're just a no-good Dakota farm girl. Not like our Canadian girls. They're better at everything." Stephen's face was twisted in a taunting leer.

She was relieved when he finally left the house. At the door, he muttered that he would be back in about a week.

"That's fine," she said tautly.

The last several weeks had been painful as hostile words flew in both directions. Their six or so years of marriage were ending, and her prospects were not good. As the daughter of a store and farm owner and then as wife of a railroad conductor, Marie was not accustomed to supporting herself, but she had thought a good deal about what she could do once she left her husband. After Stephen left, she carefully chose what to take with her: a scarf to tame her auburn curls, a jacket over three blouses and two skirts, and a modest satchel for clothing, shoes, and other necessities.

There was one more item she had to take. The slight, but strong, woman carried away a heavy box filled with treasures from the past—the vanity set from her first love, Stuart; the sterling silverware from Stephen; and other things she could not bear to leave behind.

At the train station she laid her pass on the ticket counter and requested one ticket to Calgary. She silently thanked her father for the lifetime railway pass she carried. Holding land in the Dakota Territory had endeared him to the Great Northern Railway as they built tracks across the prairie.

"Going up to see family?" The kindly ticket agent grinned at her.

"Yes, I thought I'd visit." Everyone knew Stephen was from somewhere up in Canada, and the ticket agent was not surprised at her travel plans.

As the train glided past snow-covered mountains, elk grazed on patches of grass and lakes glistened in the pale sun. Marie's thoughts drifted ahead. She had heard about the Banff Springs Hotel outside Calgary. It was considered the place to go to soak in the sulfur springs in the midst of the mountains. A pretty girl could find a job there, she reasoned. She would apply for work in the hotel's restaurant.

On her first day in the dining room, Pearl, the head waitress, began Marie's training by asking her, "Ever wait tables before, dearie?"

"No, but I've eaten at nice restaurants, so I know what good service is."

"Now, don't take me wrong, honey. We get a lot of pretty faces coming through here that can't take the guff these guys hand out."

"I can handle myself." Marie lifted her chin defiantly. Then she lowered it. "I appreciate your help, though."

"That's better." Pearl handed Marie a pile of silverware. "Fold these up in those napkins and put them there." She pointed to a pile on the table.

One of the other waitresses came around the corner, shaking her bobbed blond hair. "I'm Lucy. I'll help you get started."

Marie breathed deeply and realized she had lots to learn. She began wrapping silverware in linen napkins.

Had there been had been a birth announcement for little Mary Ada Fisher in the Somerset, Ohio, newspaper, in July 1888, it would have read something like this:

> Born this day, July 5, 1888, was a tiny little girl at the home of John and Almeda Cotterman Fisher. She was named Mary Ada by the happy parents. Welcoming this new addition to the family were her brothers, Charles, age 2, Burl, age 5, and Herbert, age 8. Mother and daughter are doing fine. She was baptized at the Somerset Lutheran parish church.

Home for Mary's first ten years was a small house outside Somerset. Life was reasonably uneventful during those early years on the family farm, but the national economy was unsettled, and many people began to look to the new land out west for relief. In 1898 the Fisher family joined neighbors to ride in boxcars on the "immigrant" train provided by Jim Hill on the Northern Pacific Railroad as they relocated to the Dakota Territory.

Homesteading required establishing a residence and living there for several years and tilling the land. The Fishers' first home was a one-room "soddy" with a tin roof and no windows. The children slept in a loft above the twenty-foot by twenty-foot room. Mary and Charlie helped their mother tend the garden while her dad and older brothers cut logs for firewood. The Fisher family held strong Lutheran values and attended church as regularly as possible. Skilled in animal care, her father was often called on to help with ailing animals, while his wife's abilities were valued as a midwife. Several years later, Mary's father opened the Fisher Mercantile Store and Post Office. The children had received several years of education in Ohio before moving west and continued their schooling in a back room of the store. They also spent a good deal of time helping with the chores that were required to manage a homestead and store.

As a teenager Mary adopted the name Marie because she felt it better suited her stature as the "most beautiful girl in Wolf Creek." She was betrothed at age sixteen, but for unknown reasons the marriage between Marie Fisher and Stuart Mahaffey did not take place on August 25, 1904, in Rugby, North Dakota, as planned.

The following year a twenty-four-year-old Canadian freight conductor for the Great Northern Railway caught Marie's eye, and she married Stephen J. Law on November 12, 1905, in Grafton, North Dakota. That same day her favorite brother, Charlie, two years her elder, married a woman named Nora in Minot.

Details of the Laws' early marital life are unknown; however, the 1910 U.S. Census shows Marie and Stephen living in Neche, North Dakota. She was a housewife and he worked for the railroad. Exactly when or why Marie left her husband is not known.

As a separated or divorced woman in 1910, Marie's future would have been uncertain, but soon thereafter she would find the job at the hotel restaurant in Banff, Canada, and begin life anew.

The days went by quickly for Marie in her new life. Her fellow waitress, Lucy, was about Marie's age, and Pearl had taken a motherly liking to them both. Marie learned from watching them work, and in her off hours, she went exploring. The hotel was surrounded with tall, heavily wooded mountains. Inside she noted that well-dressed men and gorgeous women dined there nightly, along with rough men from all over the country. The women were prettily made up and had exquisite taste in clothing and jewelry. In the dining room customers often talked about Alaska and its gold rush. Strong young male diners spoke excitedly about stampedes and new mines, filling the room with noisy exuberance.

One day Lucy commented, "You know, I might try my luck in Alaska. I've heard there're a lot of rich men up there." She tossed her head, curls shaking all over. "After all," she said, "I could make a lot more money there than I can here waiting tables. Besides, I'm getting tired of being pinched and not being paid for it." She winked at Marie, who was already thinking about the wide-open Alaska territory for herself.

But before any trip to Alaska could be made, she had a surprise visit from her husband, Stephen, who had located her at the hotel. Their confrontation turned ugly, and her employer called the sheriff. An irate Marie told the sheriff, "This man was my husband, but we're divorced; I want him to leave me alone. He's threatened me so many times, I'm scared of him. I had to leave or he would have hurt me. He hit me a couple of times." She looked so sincere and frightened, and so beautiful, the sheriff was convinced, especially since Stephen was a tall, imposing man. Outside his office the sheriff told Stephen to go on home and leave well enough alone. The discussion lasted a long time, but finally Stephen put on his hat and left.

Marie knew that part of her life was over. She was on her own, but she had made new friends. Pearl advised her to stay in Banff for a time to save money before going to Alaska, and Marie agreed. After Stephen's visit, Marie got in the habit of stopping by to see the sheriff, read his newspaper, and have a cup of coffee. His son Willy was often there, and Marie and Willy became friends. Over lunch one day, she admitted to Willy that she was getting restless.

"Hey, girl, marry me, and I'll take care of you." He threw his arm around her shoulders.

She pulled herself free. "Thanks, Willy. That's sweet of you, but that's not the answer for me."

Willy continued to hang around the sheriff's office to have coffee with Marie, or he arrived at the hotel when she got off work to walk her home. She could tell his father approved of their relationship, and this made her uneasy.

Marie kept reading about Alaska in the newspapers and noticed ads for work in the gold mines. As she listened to the talk at the hotel, her own gold fever became stronger. Waiting tables didn't pay enough, and Marie was tired of it. She had been able to save money, but it would not go far. She was determined to find a way to live well, travel, and have fun; and becoming a dance hall girl, or even a prostitute, was not a new idea. Marie had thought about it. A girl could easily earn $300 a month that way, but it had never before been real. As she considered her circumstances, lack of work experience, skills, and education, she knew that she had few other opportunities to make good money.

In the early 1900s few occupations were available to a single woman. A divorced woman was considered "fallen" and undesirable for marriage. She could do low-paying menial work and generally expect to have to endure poverty and people looking down on her, or she could set herself up in business, which frequently meant prostitution and people looking down on her.

Wherever there were large numbers of men on the frontier, a swarm of women followed to set up a line of tents, or "cribs." The women tracked down the mining towns, construction sites, military outposts, cattle terminals, supply stations, and the larger urban centers on the frontier.

Marie had written her family that Stephen had died, thinking it would invite fewer questions later on; and before she could go north, she received a letter from her brother Charles. "Herb is being discharged from the navy, and he'll be coming this way," he wrote. "Why don't you meet us in Montana? I'll bring Nora." It had been years since Marie had seen her family, and she especially appreciated being involved in a family get-together. As a special treat they had a studio picture taken in Great Falls of the four of them to celebrate being together.

Marie knew she was moving on. And she was sure it would be to Alaska, so she asked Nora and Charlie to keep her box of treasures for her, telling them, "I brought a box of things I value and I'd hate to lose track of them. I plan to travel a bit . . . I want to see the Orient, maybe go to Alaska, go around the Horn, who knows where . . . "

When she returned to Canada, Willy began to pressure Marie to marry him. Marie tried to put him off. "I'm not ready to settle down," she told him.

Concerned that Willy's father, the sheriff, might make things difficult for her if she tried to leave town, she decided to quietly take her leave. She packed hurriedly one night so she could be gone before Willy woke up the next morning.

Marie asked her friend Lucy if she wanted to join her on her Alaska adventure, but Marie had seen a young man hanging around Lucy's tables and knew Lucy had other things on her mind. She went alone to the railway station where she laid her railway pass and her latest earnings on the counter and told the clerk, "I want to go to Alaska. How far can I get on this?"

The man told her, "I 'spect you can get to Juneau."

Located on the mainland of southeast Alaska, Juneau was a bustling boomtown. Gold had been discovered across the channel in 1882, and the Treadwell and Ready Bullion mines continued to beckon men seeking their fortunes. Most of them were young, able-bodied, and alone. They had to deal with long hours, danger, fatigue, and, most of all, loneliness.

On the frontier the "sporting girls," as the prostitutes were often called, were extremely independent women with vast courage and stamina. Often they provided the major social center for the community. Many of the women also darned socks, sewed buttons back on shirts, and nursed an ill or injured man back to health, as well as providing pleasures of the flesh. Even though hardly any of the ladies of the church or married women spoke to the girls, there was a good deal of the live-and-let-live attitude in Alaska. Women from both sides had to depend on one another in times of disaster or need.

It is likely that the attractive twenty-four-year-old Marie began her career in Alaska as a dance-hall girl. Dancing came easily to her, and she soon learned how to invite men to buy her drinks. The more men she danced with, the more money she could make. Marie was petite, with auburn hair that framed her youthful face, and she had social graces that would charm men from the Alaskan legislature in addition to the rougher men from the mines. Often, it seemed that the entire Alaskan legislature was at the dance hall on Saturday nights. The decision to make even more money—through prostitution—was a step that Marie would soon take.

As the heavy traffic of the gold rush was slacking off and the reforms of the Progressive Movement were forcing prostitution underground, Dell decided it was time to leave Alaska. She would always remember her time in Alaska fondly, full of so many adventures and interesting people. It was about Juneau that she later proudly told friends, "I made $10,000 one year." She was already a good businesswoman who was aware how to make and keep customers, careful with her money, and not a user of drugs. Along with her friend Bessie Housley, Dell headed for Seattle, the first American seaport along the southbound steamship line from Alaska.

As her professional life progressed, Marie tried out several different names before settling on Dell Burke. However, when she went home to her family, she was Marie Fisher Law, the widow. It was the beginning of Marie secretly living a double life with different names and different identities.

After sightseeing, shopping, and visiting family (her older brother Herb and his family lived in Seattle), Marie made plans to visit her brother Charles and his wife, Nora, in Geraldine, Montana. Bessie began to long to see her own parents again, and the two parted, planning to meet in Butte, which was a growing boom area.

"I'm coming to Montana," Marie happily wrote her favorite brother. Charles was delighted when she arrived, and Marie was pleased to see him so happy. His life seemed to be going very satisfactorily—a baby on the way and business thriving. It was a pleasure to catch up on family news, too.

But Marie was also busy planning for the future. She could catch a train from Geraldine to Butte, meet Bessie there, and check it out. Life was becoming more predictable, so Marie took the special things that Charles and Nora had been storing for her when she headed to Butte to meet up with Bessie.

Butte was everything Dell and Bessie had expected. With almost as much bustling action as in Alaska and with the same sort of raw adventurous males roaming the streets, it was a perfect place for a girl to work. What gold had been to Alaska and California, copper was to Butte—the lifeblood of the city and the state.

In Seattle Bessie and Dell had heard that the larger houses in Butte were as elaborately decorated as the better ones in San Francisco and New Orleans. Walking along Butte's tenderloin section, they noticed that large stylish houses sat alongside small ones, and down the narrow alleys were the tiny, squalid "cribs" where some prostitutes worked. An established house was more appealing, and they soon found one where their expertise was welcome.

Although there was no direct link between the red-light district of Butte and the copper-mining companies, prostitution and other forms of vice ultimately benefited the companies. One tall office building in Butte held business offices, conference rooms, and bedrooms where a tired executive could take a nap. Often the businessmen would install Dell and other girls in the top story, where the sleeping rooms were. Dell and Bessie would occasionally ride up in the elevator with modestly dressed women who had no idea their husbands would soon be "resting" upstairs with the girls.

Life in Butte was not all work. One day when the weather was warm, the skies were clear, and business had been unseasonably slow, their madam surprised them by suggesting, "Why don't we take a break this weekend? There's an exquisite little resort hotel north of Butte where we could go for a short vacation." The madam smiled and added, "We could all use a change of pace."

Dell packed her most elegant dresses. At the resort that evening, the weather was pleasant, and Dell leisurely dined with the other girls on a balcony filled with finely dressed ladies and gentlemen. Later, she and Bessie walked to the ladies' room and passed two other guests in the entry. The women greeted the girls with a smile, and one asked, "How are you this evening?"

Dell smiled graciously. "We're fine, thank you. Isn't this weather great?"

As the girls went on inside, the women agreed and resumed their conversation. One said in a hushed voice, "I hear there are . . . you know . . . that there are all kinds of 'ladies of ill repute' here this weekend."

"No!" the other woman responded, sounding scandalized. "You don't say."

"Yes, isn't that horrible?"

"Just disgraceful . . . "

When her twin nieces were born, Marie went to Geraldine, Montana, to see the tiny girls and was delighted to visit with her brother and sister-in-law there. She asked Charles about his business and learned he now dealt with lumber and coal. She was excited to see what Charles had going on. Yes, she thought looking at her brother with his growing family, he really has it all together.

But once she was back in Butte, it was business as usual—

entertaining men and being entertained by men. One such man was tall, handsome, rich, and from a ranch near Dickinson, North Dakota. Dell enjoyed his company, and she was delighted when he arranged dates outside the house. Most men wanted one thing, which happened only in the house. But this man seemed to enjoy her company, and he had taken her out several times. One evening after dinner they strolled along the street for a while. When they reached the depot, the man reached in his pocket, pulled out tickets, and said, "Let's go."

"Go where?"

"We're going back home to Dickinson. We're gonna get married."

"Oh no, we aren't!" Dell exclaimed.

Before he could stop her, she ran to a policeman standing nearby and said, "Please make this man stop harassing me. I'm from the Washington Suite in the hotel over there."

The policeman immediately recognized the name of the hotel suite and sized up the situation. He laid his hand on the rancher's arm and told him, "Leave the lady alone, mister. Just go on home."

The rancher was angry and retorted, "But I paid the madam a whole lot for this girl and I want to take her home with me . . . " At once, the policeman grabbed the man's arm and hustled him onto the train.

Dell sighed with relief. As she told Bessie later, "I don't know if he ever got his money back from the madam, but you know what? I don't really care. I think that was a dirty trick of them both." She never saw him at the hotel again.

In January 1916, when copper prices rose to twenty cents a pound and more than fourteen thousand miners received a raise of twenty-five cents a day, an extra $6,000 was loaded into the local economy daily. The red-light district exploded with activity. At the same time, the reforms of the Progressive Movement, which had begun five years earlier, were steadily moving westward. The city fathers of Butte had tried to stop liquor sales inside the district, but they were discouraged by a system of tunnels that connected most of the major hotels and businesses in downtown Butte. Designed to carry water for the city but no longer used, the tunnels served as convenient corridors for transporting liquor and drugs and provided clandestine pathways for cautious customers.

Dell worried about Bessie, who was using laudanum and heroin regularly. Many prostitutes used these drugs to ward off pain or depression or loneliness, and she had seen many of them die, some by accident and some on purpose. Dell had heard that there was a huge dope ring that ran from Butte to Casper, Wyoming, so she was not surprised that Bessie could easily find a supplier. She tried to get her to stop using, but nothing seemed to work.

Dell was an avid reader who kept up with local and international news. She knew that part of her professional effectiveness was her ability to discuss current affairs intelligently with customers. It also helped to know what was going on in order to survive the changing times across the nation.

In December 1917 Congress passed the Webb resolution to submit to the states a national Prohibition amendment. Because of the close ties between alcohol sales and prostitution, many girls moved out of Butte in search of more tolerant surroundings elsewhere.

Dell and Bessie moved into the controversial environment of the Sandbar district in Casper, Wyoming, where production of oil, or "black gold," as some called it, had begun in 1895 with the opening of a refinery by the Pennsylvania Oil and Gas Company. Oil shipping led to an increase in rail access into Casper, and by 1915 life in Casper accelerated rapidly. By 1917 land in the Sandbar region of Casper was prime location for cheap development. Red-light businesses clustered there, along with gambling and drinking places, and the Sandbar thrived. New residents lured to town by the possibility of getting rich included carpenters, bakers, drillers, roughnecks, and teamsters along with gamblers, call girls, and confidence men.

Without a city building code, cribs and houses, eating places, and bars were built wherever new owners wished. Narrow paths were lined with cribs. During this period, girls from the Sandbar were routinely hauled into court on charges of operating or working in a house of ill repute. To make bail, the girls posted bonds up to $100. If they did not appear in court, they forfeited the bond, but all continued working. Paying the bond became part of their business overhead.

The women had not been living in the Sandbar district long before a telegram arrived for Dell saying that her mother had fallen and was very ill with diabetes. Dell's heart thudded heavily as she digested the news from her Uncle William Fisher. "I've got to go see Mama while I can," she told Bessie. She would always be glad she had made that trip home then.

On November 11, 1918, residents of the Sandbar held one of their biggest parties ever to celebrate the end of World War I. Liquor flowed freely throughout the Sandbar, despite Wyoming's decision to be "dry." Military men mingled with local residents. Glasses clanked and parties went on all night in the Sandbar. Tables, beds, and chairs were seldom empty of visitors wishing for a receptive ear.

Business had boomed all year, and Dell had used the opportunity to make a number of contacts, not only with other girls and madams but also with moonshine suppliers. Pressure was building in Casper as the city council moved to clean up the city. The Sandbar was a major target, and the council had plans to enforce the abolition of liquor sales, prostitution, and gambling. Rumors indicated arrests of anyone either frequenting the Sandbar or operating any of these businesses there would be made

Dell could feel the pressure. Bessie could, too, and her dope use increased. Sometimes she used laudanum, but frequently she used heroin.

"That stuff will wreck you," Dell reminded her.

"Not before it makes me happy," was the lackluster reply.

"I wish you wouldn't use it."

"Try it and you'll understand." Bessie held out her supply.

"No! I don't want any part of that." Dell pushed Bessie's hand away. "There's new drilling going on in the Lance Creek oil fields. That could be a good place to go. You coming with me?"

"Where? Why?"

"We've got to get out of here before they really come down on us."

"Count me in," Bessie said shrugging her shoulders indifferently.

Dell had already begun laying plans for their next move.

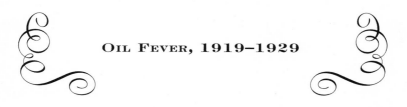

OIL FEVER, 1919–1929

Oil Fever, they called it. And Wyoming had it bad. Oil strikes around Casper came first, followed by gushers in Lance Creek about a hundred miles to the east. By fall of 1918 a dozen companies from various parts of the world were involved. Then the Fever came to Lusk, thirty miles south of Lance Creek.

Population estimates for Lusk vary from two thousand to ten-thousand during this period. Lower figures were recorded by the U.S. Census Bureau; higher estimates were based on the size of the tent village. Hotels were full, rooming houses were full, and private homes were, too. Tents provided housing for many newcomers arriving in mid-November 1918. The train depot was at the north end of the booming frontier town. New businesses and houses were springing up along the unpaved main street.

The women soon found a tent and went into business across from the depot. The following month they rented a house and signed up for utilities using names Dell was trying out, such as Della, and sometimes Delle. Later she settled on Dell. Her Canadian-born friend had already chosen hers—Bessie Housley, although she also went by Deffy Bess.

"Boy, we got out of Casper just in time, didn't we?" Bessie said as she glanced at the Casper paper.

"We knew it meant trouble when those city councilmen passed an ordinance declaring war on 'vice'—meaning everyone on the Sandbar." Dell smoothed her auburn curls into place.

"Yeah, they said they'd arrest anybody selling liquor or who was an 'inmate of houses,' if there was any sort of 'disorderly' behavior," Bessie said sarcastically. "Shoot, the men coming in from the fields were a lot more disorderly than we were."

"I know." Dell smiled. "But *they* don't."

Every day brought more exciting news. The pipeline from the Lance Creek oil field was completed, and new gushers were coming in. Mining in the Silver Cliff hill on the west side of Lusk was yielding potentially high-grade uranium. Radium held promise as a cure for all sorts of illnesses, from high blood pressure to cancer. Young and vital men flooded in from Oklahoma and other states to work in the oil fields and mine. These men possessed money and the energy to use it, and Lusk had places where they could spend it.

"There's a house for sale across from the depot with five bedrooms upstairs and a room downstairs where we could serve liquor. We could use that until we can get a real hotel."

Dell bit her lower lip and waited for Bessie's response, which was, "They already call it Girlie Street, so why not?"

"I've heard that." Dell smiled. "But I don't think they mean us. Almost all the families who live along here have all girls."

On January 3, 1919, Dell and Bessie met with Burt and

Mildred Hancock to discuss buying two lots and a building across from the depot. They settled on a price of $2,700. They continued to work out of their rented house until the house on First Street was ready. Both women had saved their money for this day, and each put into the new project what they could. Dell had a larger share and felt satisfaction that her careful management of money had made the purchase possible.

In late October 1919 the Volstead Act to enforce the 18th Amendment was passed despite President Woodrow Wilson's veto. This amendment prohibited all import, export, transport, sale, and manufacture of intoxicating liquors, thus beginning Prohibition nationwide.

January 5, 1920, was a special day for Dell as she sat in the lawyer's office with Bessie and the Hancocks. Dell was excited by the prospect of owning her own place. Shared with Bessie, yes, but her name—Dell Burke—was on the title. She was going into business in her own place.

The property on First Street included a modest two-story wood building with five bedrooms upstairs and a living or reception room and a kitchen-dining room downstairs.

The double garage would easily convert into a dance hall with a driveway leading around to the back where cars could be parked discreetly.

Dell was pleased with her business prospects in Lusk. Together with Bessie, she gathered menus from restaurants and information about obtaining girls to work for them. Setting up the house was a big step, one Dell had been looking forward to for a long time. There would be live music with excellent food, and Dell and Bessie talked with local bootleggers to see who made clean whiskey.

As the girls talked about their plans one evening, Dell longingly said, "I wish we could fix this place up really grand like some of those lovely houses in Butte and Denver and . . ."

Bessie's lower lip trembled as she responded, "You want so much."

"I do, because I want it to be really nice," Dell said wistfully. "We'll get there. It'll take us a while, but we'll make our place stand out." Dell was thoughtful for a moment. "And you know something else? There don't seem to be nearly as many problems with the law here as there were in Casper."

"That's good for us," Bessie agreed.

But when Wyoming Governor Carey appointed Sheriff A. S. Roach of neighboring Wheatland as state commissioner of Prohibition at the end of December 1919, it spelled trouble for Dell and Bessie. The *Lusk Herald* and *Van Tassell Pioneer* noted that the state superintendent of the Anti-Saloon League was highly pleased with the appointment.

It was almost public recognition for Dell and Bessie when the sheriff appeared at their door. Sounding apologetic, he told them, "Ladies, I've got to read you this summons. You're being arrested for running an illegal business." Dell had to smile at his obvious discomfort.

While the local newspaper carried nothing about their first Lusk court appearance, it still stood out as a public announcement that Bessie and Dell were in business when they were hauled into court along with other madams. The Lusk Police Docket chronicled the event this way:

TOWN OF LUSK VS BESSIE HOUSLEY, MADGE DAWSON, GENEVA GIBSON, AND DELLE BURKE

"Now on Jan. 26, 1920, at 2 p.m., comes W. F. Gardner Town Marshall, who being first duly sworn, upon his oath gives the court to understand that the Defendants are accused of the crime or offense of Maintaining a Disorderly House, all contrary to the form of the Ordinance in such case made and provided and against the peace and dignity of the Town of Lusk and the State of Wyoming. Defendants each came into court and entered a plea of 'Guilty' and court fined each one $100.00 and costs taxed in the sum of $4.35—making a total of $104.35 each and each defendant paid the same and were discharged."

[Signed] O. E. A. Blenkarn, Police Judge

This was the first of many such court appearances Dell would make over the next ten years. Appearances in court were costly, but they did not prevent Dell from staying in business. Several girls were charged monthly with being inmates of disorderly houses and fined $10 plus court costs each.

Meanwhile, Bessie was becoming increasingly nervous and moody. She slept through nights when Dell could have used her help, and other nights she was careless about her work. By March 1920 she no longer worked at all. Dell knew she couldn't keep her friend in Lusk much longer.

"Time for me to move on. Gettin' restless, I guess," Bessie said one cold day. "Hardly any business these days. You won't miss me."

Dell was not surprised, but she hated to see her leave. Bessie was her closest friend and companion, on top of being a good employee. Dell was also concerned that Bessie was not healthy. Bessie's use of laudanum had started because of an injured back, but now she used it for everything.

"I wish you wouldn't leave. We've been together for a long time, and I don't know what I'll do without you . . . "

"You're good at the business. You won't miss me." Bessie's eyes were teary.

"You will write?" Dell could hardly admit what Bessie's leaving meant to her. "And you will come back, won't you?"

"Sure, I'll be back. And I'll write and let you know where I am. You be sure to answer."

The letters came regularly at first but became less frequent as time passed. Girls and madams came and went in this business. It was hard to make close friends and harder to keep them nearby. Dell could only hope Bessie would return.

Almost every frontier town had cribs and houses of prostitution with varying reputations. Across Wyoming brothels like the Green House in Riverton, the Mag Jess House near Buffalo, several houses in Rawlins, cribs and houses on the Casper Sandbar, and the Ritz Hotel in Thermopolis were the scenes of civil disorder, knifings, fights, maulings of the girls, and drunken rages acted out in abuse or murder.

At other houses brothel keepers such as Madams Etta, Lola, and Cassie from Cody, and Maggie Wheelock in Douglas made a name for themselves with public service, donations to charitable causes, and involvement in helping in the community during local crises. Madam Sadie in Worland provided food and nursed the sick and infirm. Etta's

Crimson Way House in Cody kept high standards for its girls and their clientele. The Cozy Club in North Park required neat and clean dress for entry.

Most houses were connected with gambling, and all served alcoholic beverages. These issues alone brought trouble with the law, and madams were frequently arrested. Their regular contribution to the city assured them of the privilege of operating and provided free advertising.

Dell had learned that successful madams faced the challenge of being both hostess and businesswoman. The way she presented herself set the tone for her house and determined the quality of her customers. She chose not to drink alcoholic beverages with customers, and she allowed no drunken girls or customers in her place.

"Hey, Luke," the rancher called out to a ranch hand after they finished their business on a Friday afternoon. "Meet me at the hotel for a drink?"

Luke nodded. Only one kind of hotel in town offered alcohol. "Which one?"

"Dell serves clean whiskey."

"Suits me."

Four or five other men sat around small tables sipping drinks when Luke and Hal walked in. The house was decorated in lush decadence. Dell had found resources for brocades, velvets, and silks that lined the windows and covered the sofa and chairs.

"Well, if it isn't Hal. I wondered when you'd discover this place." Good-natured kidding floated back and forth.

"Your wife won't miss you none?" asked one.

"Nah," Hal said, "she knows I come here for a drink every so often. The girls only serve drinks this hour anyway."

"Oh hey, Hal, did you hear about Sheriff Joss?" Hal shook his head as the lanky rancher bent over with laughter and began his story. "The other day, he confiscated a batch of whiskey one of my neighbors had out at his house. Seems that the sheriff put it in a cell in the old jail and he got called out, and you know what happened?"

"What's that?"

The rancher took another swig of whiskey. "Well, while he was out, the ranchers come in town, put masks on their faces, and tied Mrs. Joss up in the kitchen upstairs where she was fixing dinner. Then, they made off with the liquor before the sheriff could get back." He threw his head back and guffawed. "And the best part is the judge threw the case out of court. No evidence!"

The Chinese cook poked his head out from the kitchen, his long braid swinging behind his head. "How many, Missy Dell?" Dell counted hands, and soon venison steaks appeared on platters. She wore a dark blue velvet dress as she called the men to dinner and daintily inhaled on her cigarette in its long silver holder while she talked with them. The men feasted until after dark, when musicians began tuning their instruments and strumming chords.

"Time for me to head out. How about you, Luke?" Hal picked up his hat and turned toward the door.

"I'm gonna stay and listen a while. We don't get real music around here too often."

One of the other men turned around and spoke to Luke. "You know what kind of music Dell serves up, don't you?"

"Nah, I don't."

"It's that jazz that's played down in Orleans by them Black folks. Gets in your blood and makes you want to do all sorts of things, they say."

"Hmm," mused Luke, "now that would be right interesting. Guess I'm gonna have to listen close."

Several hours and drinks later, Luke still sat absorbing the company. With his wife in Nebraska tending a sick parent, he had no one hurrying him home. The girls danced around the floor in their short skirts, but none of them appealed to him. Finally, he called it a night. "Dell, I got to give you credit. This here is a fine way to spend Friday night."

"Thank you, Luke." Dell smiled. "Come back and see us again." A number of men and women were regular drink and dinner customers on Fridays and Saturdays. The lively jazz music was fun for everyone.

In October 1920 the town of Lusk installed water meters. Dell's connection cost $7.50. The monthly assessment for water usage changed from $8.00 per month to a figure that ranged from $3.40 to $11.08.

It had been a busy year, with four houses employing at least seven girls. "Business was booming. The money was plentiful, and so were women, booze and gambling," Dell later commented to a reporter.

By February 1921, the other houses along Lusk's First Street had closed down. No explanation for their closings was available. "At least there's no competition any more," Dell told her girls as they came home from paying their fines at the courthouse. "It's an expensive way to get police protection, but they come whenever we get a rowdy we want help with." She shook the snow out of her auburn curls.

She had called on her attorney friend on the way home from the courthouse. A large book lay open on his desk when she entered. "What's the worst they could do to me?" she asked him. "This monthly $100 fine is outrageous."

"Actually, it could be worse. According to the Wyoming statutes, you could be fined as much as $200 and imprisoned in the county jail from one to six months." He tapped the page in front of him. "They could also slap you with more fines for each day you operate after they charge you."

Dell sighed. "I'm glad they don't do that." She continued to support Lusk as its only recognized madam, paying $100 plus costs at each court appearance. No jail time was ever added. March was her busiest month, when four girls worked for her; most of the rest of the year, one girl was in court with her.

Diversions from running the brothel came in a variety of ways, including spending time with Artie Johnson, Jerry Dull, and Duff Hollon, who were among the young men who worked at Mike Vollmer's garage.

Jerry and his friends often hung out at the brothel in the evenings. "You know," he told Dell, "you have the best whiskey and music in town. On top of the best-looking dance partners." The mild-mannered young man was handy at fixing things, and Dell was pleased to have his help.

Always a private person, Dell rarely talked with the girls about her family, but when she received the telegram telling her of the death of her mother, a couple of regulars were on hand. As she ripped open the envelope, Peggy watched closely. "Who's it from?"

"My Uncle William. Mama passed away September 29. It's not really unexpected." Dell paused to wipe her eyes. "She was almost seventy years old. They'll bury her there in Rolette. Near the old family place. Mama was really sick when I visited a couple years ago. I'm glad I went out then 'cause I can't go now. With this our busy season, I just can't leave." Dell sighed. It was just the first of a number of family events she would have to miss, and her heart ached with the loss.

Dell furnished her place attractively with features she was proud of—fine furnishings and paintings, beautiful clothing for her and the girls, excellent food, and live music nightly. It wasn't always easy to find a band willing to come to the frontier, but Dell had connections. The music made the hotel a lively place, although nationwide jazz was called "devil's music" and was associated with vulgar behavior. Therefore, jazz was excluded from decent concert halls and only brothels featured it. When this belief made its way to Lusk, the mayor decreed that live music would not be permitted in any entertainment places in town. The musicians fled in the face of incarceration.

As she sipped coffee with the cook in a local cafe, Dell couldn't help but complain. "What am I going to do? Live music brought people in and now I can't have any."

The cook thought it over. "You know, I have an old player piano you could have for $25. It takes a quarter for each play."

Dell was delighted. She moved the player piano into the hotel, and it was a hit. "You know, that player piano brings in more money than the girls do. At $100 a night, that's about four hundred plays—one tune for a quarter—that's six hours and forty minutes solid music," she told friends. Dell always appreciated finding ways to make money and at the same time satisfy customers.

In January 1922 Dell received devastating news from Montana. Her favorite brother, Charlie, had gone to Great Falls to buy restaurant equipment and never returned. At first his wife had thought he was delayed, but it was unlike him not to let her know.

As Dell packed her suitcase, she told her girls, Peggy and Margaret, "I'm not sure when I'll get back, but if you could take over for me the rest of this month, Margaret, and you two could split the load for the next couple of months, it would help me."

"Sure, we'll handle it for you."

"My little dogs won't be a bother. There's enough food in the kitchen to hold them while I'm gone, and here's some cash if they need anything else."

"We'll take care of them for you," Peggy said, cradling one of the small brown Pekingese dogs. "What do you think happened?"

"Nobody knows. No problems I know of. He was happy with his business to the best of my knowledge, and their kids were doing fine." Dell was perplexed.

"You said he was a good businessman," Margaret remembered.

"He had a knack with people and a good business head. I can't believe someone did anything to him, but I just don't know . . . " Tears filled her eyes as she snapped her suitcase shut. "I'll get the FBI on this, and maybe we can find out what really happened."

Dell spent the next four months intensely looking for Charles. Her efforts would continue for years, but nothing ever turned up. From time to time Dell met with FBI agents to discuss her brother's disappearance. She could not understand how any man—especially one as well known and well liked as Charles Fisher had been—could suddenly and completely disappear. It did not make sense.

It made no sense to Charlie's wife, Nora, either, but she had to get on with life and tend to their five children as best she could. It was impossible to take care of all five at home, so she placed them in an orphanage for a while. While trying to pull her life back together, Nora visited her father-in-law, John Fisher, and tried to get him to move east with her. Before that could happen, he died in his sleep on November 15, 1924, at the age of seventy-four. He was buried beside his wife in the North Dakota cemetery. This was a low point for the Fisher family, aggravated by the problems facing the rest of the nation.

Nationwide, the economy was sagging. Monthly court fines for operating a disorderly house dropped from $100 in January 1922 to $50 the following month, and a year later they were set at $25. Court costs were generally $4.35. From January 1920 through June 1929, Dell was regularly charged with violating the "City Ordinance against Maintaining a Disorderly House." This charge was later changed to City Ordinance No. 75, which encompassed making, selling, and serving alcohol, all forms of gambling, and prostitution. Fines fluctuated over the years with the rising and falling economy, ranging from $100 in 1920, $50 in 1922, $25 during 1923 to 1927, $15 in 1928, and back to $25 in 1929. Overall, Dell appeared in the Lusk Court about eighty-five times and paid more than $4,000 in fines.

Wyoming's economy was mostly rural. Friday was the day to go to town, the bank, the courthouse, or to do other business. Many people came to town once a month to buy groceries on Saturday afternoons. Some stayed on for entertainment at the movie theater or the Merry Whirl Ballroom above it, and some visited the bars, gambling houses, or brothels.

Despite the mild recession men from the oil fields still rolled into town on Saturday nights. Having worked hard all week and being young, vigorous, and lonely, they sought places to spend that energy, and a house of prostitution provided it. On a typical Saturday night, men slouched on the sofa sipping drinks with the girls before heading upstairs. But on some nights atypical events occurred, such as the one described here. Horse hooves pounded against the dirt street outside the hotel, and men's voices resounded. Shots rang out, and Dell glanced around nervously.

The girls began to move toward the hallway, and two men stood up. Peggy asked, "Think we should go upstairs?"

"Wait and see if they're coming in here," Dell responded quietly. Loud voices could be heard from the street.

"I think they are. Chuck and Bill wanted to see me tonight, and each thinks he's the only one." Peggy ducked her head mischievously.

"You asking for trouble?" Dell demanded as guns fired in the street outside. The sounds of scuffling and yells could be heard, and the women hurried to watch out the window.

"That's Chuck," Peggy said, "but I don't know the others."

"There's more than two out there," Dell retorted. "Turn out these lights. Everyone upstairs. I think it's safer up there." A bullet whistled by her head as she spoke. Pounding on the door, banging on the side of the house, the boys tried to find a way to get inside the hotel. Suddenly, there was the sound of shattering glass. Voices were louder now. Peggy scooted down the stairs before Dell could stop her. "Call the sheriff," Dell whispered to one of the men.

"Get outta here . . . " resounded in the hallway.

"Whaddya mean you gonna see Bill tonight? You're my girl . . . " Dell started down the stairs in time to see fists flying, and Peggy slumped to the floor.

"Stop that, young man. You get out of here. *Now!*" she commanded.

He turned toward her as the sheriff stepped inside the door, followed by a deputy.

"Okay, that's enough." The sheriff looped an arm around the young man and led him outside. A draft whipped the curtain through the broken window in the door as they left.

Dell turned toward Peggy, who was sitting up and gingerly touching her cheek, where Dell could see the dark spot on her face in the dim light.

"Let's put some ice on that." She led Peggy toward the kitchen.

In the street, when the other young men saw the sheriff, they quickly moved out. The street became quiet, and life in the hotel proceeded as usual.

The business people of Lusk probably met from time to time to discuss the issues that faced the growing town. Dell would generally have chosen not to attend, and if she did attend, she would have kept a low profile. The room would have been filled with businessmen and women, and the events might have gone like this.

A woman in a large brown hat rose from a chair near the front and said in a loud voice, "I think it's time to close down that house on First Street."

"It's bad. They play evil music and lead men to the devil," spoke up the woman beside her.

Another woman stood up. "The men go there, get drunk, go off with the girls, and . . . it's awful."

A snicker moved across the room. One of the men rose to respond, "You may be right about part of that, but where else in town can a man get a drink?" He faced the women. "Then too, we get a lot of young men coming in from the oil fields needing a place to let off steam. These guys can get rough. They cut each other up when they fight. When they go to the hotel on First Street, they leave our decent girls and women alone."

Heads nodded around the room. Another man stood up. "From what I hear, towns around here without a place like that have problems with men bothering their women."

The women continued to argue, but in the end they had to agree. "Maybe it does make it a little safer for our daughters."

"Keep your men happy, and most of them'll stay home anyway," came a soft husky voice from the back of the room.

Although Dell had not lost hope that Bessie would come back, she could not help but wonder if she would ever see her friend again. It had been some time since the last letter had arrived. When she answered the timid knock at the door one February day in 1927, Dell opened it with great joy. She grabbed Bessie, pulled her inside, and hugged her warmly. It had been a long time since she had seen her friend, and Dell held her out for inspection. "You look awfully thin. Are you all right?"

"Yeah, sure. I'm all right. I'm tired, but not too tired to work. You could use another girl, right?"

"That's right, I can always use your help."

She could not say it aloud, but Dell was concerned at seeing Bessie in this condition. It was not long before it became obvious that Bessie was quite sick. She worked until sometime during September 1927.

"I don't think you should work now." Dell put her arms around her friend. "When you get to feeling better we'll talk about it."

Bessie nodded. "I feel awful. Thanks for understanding."

"You can stay here as long as you want." Dell watched sadly as the use of dope took over Bessie's life.

As the economy continued to sag, Dell carefully observed when land taxes became delinquent. Grass and weeds on the lot east of her property indicated neglect, and on August, 2, 1927, she purchased it for only $500 because taxes had not been maintained by the former owners.

She also looked for property outside of Lusk, such as in the once-booming area of the Lance Creek oil fields in Manville, about ten miles from Lusk. "I've found a building in Manville we can move in here and set on that lot," Dell jubilantly told friends. Moving it would be less expensive than constructing a new building. The property had been a hotel with ten bedrooms upstairs and a bathroom. Just in time to expand her operation, the new building provided accommodations. Downstairs, a small room could be used for business meetings, and a large room would be perfect for dancing and reception with a bar at one end. A laundry room was on the other side of the stairs. Across the hall Dell would make her private living room, bedroom, and bathroom. The kitchen and dining room were behind those. A long hallway divided the sides of the hotel both upstairs and down. They could still the use the old building for the girls to live in.

It would be very satisfactory for Dell to have her own apartment. Now she could really make herself a home. As she unpacked the box, she looked for a place to conceal its contents. Though she no longer wanted to use them, she valued the monogrammed silverware from Stephen and the vanity set from Stuart. She found a hiding place behind the bathtub she doubted anyone would discover. Pieces of jewelry she wanted to keep went into her dresser drawer, including a small chain with a pendant marked SJL. As she pondered how to make her new hotel stand out, she decided to paint it yellow. Soon the reputation of the Yellow Hotel spread across the state and the region.

One day Dell and Bessie sat sipping coffee in the dining room of the new hotel while listening to Jerry Dull and Duff Hollon talk.

"You know, we could move supplies and machinery from Lusk to the Lance Creek oil field," Duff said thoughtfully.

Jerry nodded. "That's true. We could. Might start out with one or two trucks and get more as we go along."

"I've got an old truck we could start with. We'll put those solid rubber tires on it, so it'll carry the weight."

"We gotta find capital somewhere to get started."

It is likely that Dell volunteered to help finance the startup. By that time she was known for investing in the future of the town. Word had gotten around among ranchers and town merchants, and they often turned to her for help. She was pleased that she had been able to keep most of them in business. Almost everyone paid her back when they could.

Duff and Jerry formed the Hollon and Dull Transportation Company to haul oil-field equipment between Lusk and Lance Creek in mid-1927. It is also likely that Dell and Jerry's personal relationship was deepening even then. Dell had taken an interest in the stock market and new oil companies. Her investments varied and are not all documented. In the mid- to late-1920s, Dell bought or built a small hotel that became known as the Bungalow Hotel, which was sold and moved sixty miles away to Torrington. No additional details about this investment are known. Sometime in 1925 or 1926, she purchased five shares of Midland Piggly Wiggly Company Class A Stock and five shares of Class B Stock. In August 1929 the company sent her dividends of $3.

Even though she knew it was coming, it still hurt that bittersweet day of March 12, 1929, when Dell sat in the district court to hear Judge C. O. Brown's comments. "In consideration of your bid—it being the highest in the amount of $500—in the matter of the Estate of Bessie Housley, Deceased . . . " he droned on.

Dell shut her eyes tightly. She could still hear Bessie's plaintive voice. "You will take care of it for me. Make sure my things go to my family without them knowing anything?" Dell handed her check to Judge Brown, knowing he would forward the amount without comment except to say that Bessie had died of pneumonia. Then Dell arranged for Bessie's burial without a headstone in the Lusk cemetery at the north end of town. The grave still lies unmarked, known only to those who tend the grounds.

When a flu epidemic hit Lusk in the spring of 1929, twenty-one people died. Dell Burke and Mrs. Tom Fagan Sr., wife of a leading Lusk attorney, were among the people who pitched in to help. After the worst of the flu was over, the two women took a walk downtown. It was unusual for Dell to link arms with a local person and to appear on the street so prominently, but perhaps fighting the deadly illness together had built camaraderie between them. When Mrs. Fagan was questioned afterwards about the propriety of being seen with this companion, she told her critics, "Well, I'll walk with her wherever and whenever I want to. She's a good person."

While the nation faced depression, the Lusk-Lance Creek area experienced another moderate oil boom. In April 1928 the new Ranger Hotel heralded an era of elegance in downtown Lusk. On the main floor were the Bishop Pool and Billiard Room and the Irving Mills Hardware. A sellout crowd from around the state purchased 370 tickets in advance for the gala opening of the hotel.

However, power and water problems continued to plague Lusk. The plant was failing. Newspaper articles frequently described attempts to secure electric power from the Guernsey Dam in cooperation with the Mountain States Power Company. However, yearlong negotiations between Lusk Mayor Godfrey, the Lusk City Council, and a representative of the power company failed to produce any satisfactory conclusion. It appears that Dell, who in addition to her concern for the health of the citizens of Lusk, also took an interest in the city's progress and livelihood and met with someone from the city council to offer financial assistance sometime between the last city power-company negotiation in April and the city council meeting in June 1929. Replacement of the 200-kilowatt engine and generator was necessary for Lusk to continue providing power. (Details of this negotiation are not available; however, Dell was repeatedly credited with having underwritten the loan.)

It is no surprise that after June 11, 1929, no further charges of violating City Ordinance No. 75 were made against Dell Burke on the Lusk Police Docket. Nevertheless, demonstrating good citizenship did not protect Dell from district court proceedings already begun against her. In December 1929 Dell made front-page headline news: Abatement Suspends Operation. *The Lusk Herald and Van Tassell Pioneer* announced that the restraining order granted by District Court Judge E. H. Fourt stopped Dell Burke from operating the hotel on First Street based on her sale of liquor and the unsavory reputation the hotel had. The order effectively closed the place down for the duration of the injunction.

"Okay," Dell told her girls. "It's time for a vacation anyway."

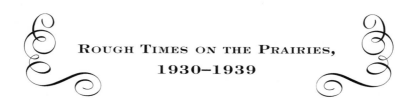

ROUGH TIMES ON THE PRAIRIES, 1930–1939

"Now, where'll I go?" Dell wailed. "I can't stay at the hotel, and who in this town'll have me?"

Jerry Dull smiled down at her. "You could stay with us. Mom likes you and you'd be welcome."

"That's a possibility. Thanks." She stirred the sugar in her coffee cup round and round.

"Look at it this way," Jerry replied, trying to sound convincing. "Most of your friends are men, and I doubt their wives would want to take you in."

"I'll talk with your mom," Dell decided. "More coffee?"

"Sure." He held out his cup. "While you're not at the hotel, me and the guys could check to make sure nobody bothers the place."

"I'd appreciate that, Jerry." He was nice looking, a friendly quiet man two years her junior. Because he had continued to hang around the hotel doing minor repairs, few people realized the depths of their discreet friendship.

In March 1930 Judge C. O. Brown approved the temporary injunction that had been granted earlier by Judge Fourt in the district court. It would be in full force until December 31, 1930, and put the hotel out of business for the year. Dell was charged with operating a resort and told she would be permitted to reenter and live at her hotel on First Street only after she provided a $1,000 bond as a guarantee that she would not violate the law.

The situation was not as humorous to Dell as it was to the young deputy whom Judge Fourt had given the special assignment of guarding the hotel—guarding it lest she return without paying the bond, she was sure. Dell packed what she knew she would need, and the deputy locked the door behind her and took his position.

A few days passed before she could pay the bond and tell the deputy, "You can leave, now." She was still smarting as she thought about the expense. The deputy smirked a little as he tipped his hat and wished her good day. At least that was over, and she could move back in soon.

"I've really appreciated your letting me stay here," Dell told Jerry and his mother that evening over dinner. "You know, since I can't do any business in the hotel for a while or I'll be in trouble, I think I will go visit my family in Ohio and Michigan."

"Ohio's where you was born, wasn't it?" Mrs. Dull asked as she cleared the table. "How long since you been there?"

"I can't remember exactly. We moved to North Dakota in 1898; then Mother and I went back two years later. Then I was in North Dakota a few years ago." Dell was thoughtful. "It'd be good to see them all, and I'll have the time."

"Wish I could go with you. Ohio's where I was born," Jerry said wistfully, "but me and Duff got business to tend to." He looked down. "Any idea when you'll be back?"

Dell heard concern in Jerry's voice. She liked knowing he cared how long she'd be gone. "I'll stay until the weather gets warmer back here," she said saucily.

"Be sure to come back."

"Don't worry. Lusk is home."

His grin spread from one ear to the other.

The visit to see her family was for both business and pleasure. Dell was considering measures to protect her property.

Dell recognized her cousin immediately as he stepped up to the train in Glenford, Ohio. "Hello, Homer!"

"Been a long time since you visited the Cotterman family. Good to have you here!" He hugged her tightly.

All the family converged on them that night for a big party celebrating Mary's return—that was the name by which this family knew her. She stayed around Somerset for some time, visiting old schoolmates, friends from years earlier, and family members. Dell observed her family while she talked with them, looking for someone she could trust. She needed someone to "front for her" in case of litigation against the hotel.

It was especially good to see Charlie's son Roy, who had moved to Detroit several years earlier to find work. He had left his family in Minnesota, where they moved after his grandfather's death in 1924. Roy looked so much like his father, it made her miss Charlie once more.

On her return to Lusk, Dell settled back into the hotel, tidying up her rooms. She immediately went to see her attorney and began to make plans. Numerous men had asked when the hotel would reopen. While the legal system had to give its official approval, at least she could start planning for the big reopening.

Late in the evening on July 24, 1930, Jerry's friend Duff banged on the hotel door while loudly calling Dell's name.

She quickly made her way down the hallway. "What is it?"

"Jerry's been hurt. He's in Casper at Memorial Hospital."

"What happened?" Dell was shocked.

"He was unloading equipment and the baler slipped off the truck. That thing weighs more than sixteen hundred pounds. It gashed him real bad."

"Where's his mom?"

"She's at the hospital. They called her 'cause he was running a high fever and they was worried about gangrene. He might lose that whole leg."

Dell recovered herself. "Want to come in and have a cup of coffee?"

Duff nodded and sank gratefully into a chair in the kitchen as Dell heated coffee in the pot.

"How'd it happen?" she asked.

"He was hauling this baler out to the Midwest refinery west of Casper, and it slid off the truck. Crushed his foot and busted bones all up and down his leg. It took twenty stitches to close it up. It looked awful."

The next several months were a blur to Dell. Between visiting Jerry in Casper, planning where he would live when he left the hospital, and generally preparing to reopen the hotel, the time passed quickly. Before he could come home, Jerry had to be moved to the hospital in Denver for further operations. By October 1930 he was back from Denver, where his foot had been removed to save his leg. He would have to wear a prosthesis, but he was expected to be able to walk again.

His mother worried. "I can't really take care of him as much as he's going to need. Think you could manage him there at the hotel, Dell?"

"Sure, and when I'm not around, the girls could help out. That way, I can keep an eye on him and make sure he does what the doctor says. Come visit any time."

Jerry was not an easy patient. As his leg healed, he became irritable and anxious to be more active. "I can't haul supplies anymore," he told Dell angrily, downing the glass of whiskey she held out to him to ease the pain.

"For now, you need to rest and let your leg heal," she advised.

"I'm forty years old. Can't work. No money. I don't know what I'm gonna do."

"There's always something . . . " Dell began. She had been through enough to know there were always ways to make a living.

Jerry had a hard time seeing it her way, and he often found whiskey eased both the pain caused by his leg and by his having to give up his partnership in the dray company. Jerry's partner, Duff Hollon, sympathized, but he also knew a strong able body was required to move the heavy equipment; he had to find someone else to work with him.

Dell tried to keep Jerry busy as his leg healed. "Jerry, could you build a new fence in front of the hotel?"

"I s'pose so." Jerry took another swig from the bottle.

She wondered how straight the fence would be and decided she would make sure it was built properly.

"I bought the lumber for it today."

Jerry shrugged. "You must want it right away."

"That would be fine."

Somewhat grudgingly, Jerry did the work. He did a good job when he was sober, but he was often not.

Dell was disgusted, but she did not give up on Jerry. When he wasn't drinking, he was a swell companion. His mom often invited them over for dinner, and the three of them spent long evenings talking together. After his leg healed, Jerry moved back in with his mother, but he was often at the hotel helping with minor repairs or just visiting with Dell.

When the market crash of 1929 evolved into the Great Depression, it rippled across the nation and gradually reached the western states. Throughout the nation, businesses failed and banks closed by the dozens. Farm prices collapsed, and small farmers were pushed from their farms. More than one hundred thousand small businesses closed, and millions of people were unemployed. Some simply rode the rails; others moved as far west as California looking for work.

Lusk was changing too. The town's population dropped to 1,218. Yet optimism was still evident among those who held on. The Niobrara Co-operative Creamery showed off its first run of butter during an Open House, the George Lathrop Memorial monument that still marks the Cheyenne-Deadwood Stagecoach route was erected at the western edge of town, and dedication services were held for a new high school. But the national economy was not the only thing depressing the western plains states—drought conditions were creating havoc. Livestock ranchers had little or no food for their animals, and crops were poor or nonexistent. Morale plunged along with income, and, as with the rest of the nation, hard times came to Lusk. Transient men, commonly called bums or hoboes, camped by the river under the trees. Men willing to work went to people like Mrs. Frank A. Barrett, wife of a Lusk lawyer. She put them to work beating rugs and doing other chores for a few dollars.

Men also began turning to Dell for help. It was difficult to say when it started, but Dell noticed that more and more old sheepherders knocked on her back door asking if they could stay the night. There were always odd jobs for them to do. Window screens needing to be put back in place, a little paint brushed here or there, and minor repairs to make. In the spring, it was the other side of the story as ranchers appeared on the back doorstep asking, "Anyone want a job?" Someone always bounded down the stairs ready for work.

Other hungry men came to the back door, where they were given food but not allowed inside.

In these economically depressed times, Dell often provided a room for a man with little means who did not want the other hotel services. Men, including Native Americans, were sent upstairs for a soft bed in a warm room. It was against the law for her to sell Native Americans hard liquor, but she could supply breakfast as well as candy, salt, or tobacco.

Critical friends wondered, "Dell, how can you afford to do this? You'll never see these guys again."

"Maybe. I think this'll pay off in the long run," she would explain. "Wait and see."

The year 1930 was a long one. While Dell had been busy preparing to reopen the hotel, it had been hard for her to be patient. There were girls to locate. There were whiskey suppliers to bargain with. And there were other tasks to be done, like cleaning the rooms, laundering linens, making new drapes, and negotiating for food and other supplies.

"We'll soon be back in business," Dell exclaimed to Jerry one afternoon late in December. "And they better not try to close me down again!" she said with a gleam in her eye.

"How's that?" Jerry looked over at her appreciatively.

"I could always call in those bonds. You know, the ones for the power."

"You wouldn't!"

"I could." She reflected, "Good thing I had money saved back."

"More than I can say for myself," he answered sourly.

"But your leg's a lot better, and you're getting used to that prosthesis. You walk almost normal now."

"I still need a cane."

"By the time we reopen, you'll be ready to dance with me." She looked up at him. "I'm counting on that."

"Think so?"

"You know I'm throwing a big party New Year's Eve, with fireworks and everything. We'll start 1931 off right." She sounded excited. What a good way to announce the Yellow Hotel was back in business. "Come and see." She led the way into the reception room. "What do you think?"

Jerry looked it over. "Looks spiffy." He examined the bar. New glasses sparkled temptingly on the freshly polished surface. Bottles filled the rack behind the bar.

New velvet curtains draped across the windows. Western paintings and pictures decorated the walls above the comfortable sofas and chairs that lined the room. A live orchestra could easily set up in one corner of the large reception room.

It was one helluva swell party. The girls looked their best. And cost $2 a throw. Liquor flowed freely—the first drink was on the house. Dell greeted all comers with a smile. She carried a long elegant silver cigarette holder from which she occasionally pulled a stream of smoke. Dressed in the latest style, her long-waisted green pleated skirt bounced as she kept time to the music while watching her girls at work.

Minnie was young, with bobbed brown hair, and her short skirt revealed rolled-down pink silk hose above powdered knees. She scanned the crowd. When a young cowboy walked in, she walked up to him. "Hey cutie, wanna dance?"

"Aw, I'm not good at that."

"Let's get a drink first." She led him toward the bar. "How about if I teach ya the Charleston?"

After he tossed down the free drink, he stepped out on the floor for his "lesson." Feet and legs flying, soon he had the steps down. With flushed faces, they went upstairs for a quick one.

Golden blond curls framed Penny's face as she approached an older man. "What's the long face for, sad man?" She sat beside him and pulled out a cigarette, which he lit for her.

"Times sure have changed. Girls don't look the same. Music's different. Everything's new and seems strange. Don't even know how to dance anymore."

"You'll get used to it. C'mon, I'll show you how to do one of the new ones. Bet you can."

Reluctantly, he followed Penny onto the floor, and they danced as the orchestra played "Happy Times Are Here Again" and "Let's Fall in Love."

With a sheepish grin, he said, "I think I'm fallin' in love."

"Wanna find out, big boy?" She cocked her head.

"Sure, let's go upstairs."

Eventually, the railroad crews, passengers, cowboys, hunters, and servicemen all returned, with regular customers coming from throughout eastern Wyoming, western South Dakota, and Nebraska. Business was even better than it had been during Prohibition. Later historians would note that Dell's Yellow Hotel was the only first-class "Sporting Club" in the region during this period.

In the spring of 1931, Dell received a letter from her sister-in-law Nora. The Depression in Michigan, which had brought the entire family to its knees, was wearing hard on Nora. "Ready for help at the hotel?" she wrote. The children were working when they could find jobs and could stay with family members while she was in Wyoming.

Dell was pleased to hear from her sister-in-law, and Nora moved to Lusk. Although it was a bit awkward at first, Nora accepted the hotel business and pitched in to help keep the place in order. Dell especially enjoyed talking with her sister-in-law over coffee in the mornings. They both still longed to find Charles and pondered new ways to search. Nora helped cook meals and maintained the large flower and vegetable gardens.

That fall, Dell took a step she continued for years to protect her business from possible legal seizure. She warranty deeded the lots where her business and home stood to Nora Fisher.

The August 7, 1931, Niobrara County Court Record reads: "Dell Burke WD Block 4, Lots 8 & 9 to Nora Fisher for "$1.00 for the lots together with all the privileges, hereditaments, tenements and appurtenances thereunto appertaining, or in any wise belonging . . . " Dell signed herself as "widow and unmarried."

"That sounds so official," Nora exclaimed. "Does that make me liable for anything?"

"Not really," Dell assured her. "It puts my property out of reach from my creditors for the time being. Thanks for letting me do that."

"I'm glad I can help."

As the Depression continued, many men were still without jobs, even men who were willing to work. They could always use a meal, and this meant extra cooking.

"Hardly know what I'd do without you," Dell told Nora one day as they prepared food. "It's good to have you here." Nora grinned. It was refreshing for them both to be able to talk about the old times in the Fisher family together.

Early that summer, Dr. Walter Reckling moved to Lusk, and he became both an advocate for and a nemesis to Dell. As county health inspector, Doc Reckling provided regular medical checkups for Dell and her girls, but this forthright outspoken medic sometimes irritated her.

The Depression may have slowed business down some, but the biggest impact was on getting paid. "I've heard," Dell told Jerry, "that girls in Casper are lucky to get paid for their services these days and there are days they aren't. Some guys bring bread or other food."

"Well, at least they can eat that way."

Whiskey numbed some people to the bitter effects of unemployment and the seemingly endlessly depressed economy. For others it meant income . . . and survival. While they were not the only producers, ranchers in the Hat Creek Breaks north of Lusk found their land ideal for making moonshine. During these bleak times, it was the only cash crop for many of them. Steep hills covered with dark ponderosa pines full of nooks and crannies made a still easy to hide and hard to find. Nearby prairies provided usable grain.

Corn became the standard for whiskey, partly because it was a readily available crop. In addition, even dry-land homesteaders began to raise corn, rye, or wheat, any of which could produce large enough quantities to supply a still and not be too obvious. Some families in the hill country who survived those years on moonshine income stopped making it when the economy became more stable.

Moonshiners delivered their products to the Yellow Hotel in containers that ranged from crocks to large milk cans. She found sources for the smaller bottles by appealing to young entrepreneurs. "Okay, boys. Bring me pop bottles, old whiskey bottles, any bottle I can use to put whiskey in, and I'll pay you for them," she would tell the group that gathered at the back door of the hotel. "The bottles need to be in good shape, but we can clean them up."

When the boys came back with hands full of bottles, she counted out their pay carefully. "That's five cents a bottle," she told them. She enjoyed talking with these bright-eyed energetic youngsters.

Throughout this period moonshiners knew that the Yellow Hotel was a good market for their products. Fred Bryan and Jess Boner were two of Dell's favorite whiskey producers. She knew they were careful to use only copper tubing and avoided anything that had lead in it lest it make the drink poisonous.

One day when her supply was getting low, she called one of her suppliers. "Fred, could you bring me a few gallons of whiskey?"

"Sure."

At the same time, she was concerned for his safety. He was in as much danger of being arrested for carrying liquor as she was for serving it. "You be careful now. The Feds are watching my place and I don't want you to be caught."

He drove his horses down the alley behind the building as

planned and glanced over at the little coalhouse behind it. The glint of eyeglasses shone through a crack between the boards, so he drove on past.

Parking the horses in front of the building, he reached in the buggy, pulled out several gallons of whiskey, and carried them up to the front door.

When he knocked, Dell cracked the door open. "How'd you get up here? How'd you get past those Feds? I know they're watching me." Dell quickly pulled him inside.

Fred grinned. "I know, but they're only watching the back. They ain't watching the front door."

With money tight to nonexistent, many landowners fell delinquent on mortgage payments and taxes. Always on the lookout for a good investment both for herself and to benefit the town, Dell began to consider buying a piece of reclaimed property outside town in the fall of 1931.

"Hey Jerry, guess what I found today?" she said, excitedly pulling off her jacket.

"What's that?"

"I just discovered a property two miles east of town that was sold for back taxes, and it's up for sale."

"How much do they want for it?"

"We just started talking about it, but I can begin the purchase process by paying $13.83," said Dell. "The rest of the payments bring the total price to approximately $2,513."

"That's not bad."

"That would give us a place to have privacy for all of us. And perhaps we can use it for special parties later on."

"I could put a table in the basement for games." Jerry scratched his head.

"Lots of possibilities."

During this time the rules with which she operated the Yellow Hotel were taking shape. These rules would keep the hotel quietly in operation for the next four decades. The hotel closed at midnight Monday through Saturday, and it stayed shut on Sundays. Rowdiness was not tolerated. While intimacy was provided inside the hotel, discretion was observed on the outside.

As the year drew to a close, Nora wanted to be back with her family. Once more, legal papers were drawn up. On December 18, 1931, Nora warranty deeded the lots to one of Dell's trusted friends, Francis Day.

It had been a good year together, but it had to end. "I'll miss you, Nora." Dell knew her sister-in-law was homesick for her children and family.

Back home, the Depression continued to plague the economy. Nora's son Roy was out of work and restless. When Dell heard about it, she decided to put him to work at the country place and sent money for him to come to Wyoming.

"I know how to do all sorts of things," he told Dell. "I'm good with a hammer and a lawn mower."

"What sort of work have you done?"

"After Dad disappeared . . . " His voice faltered for a moment. "I took different kinds of jobs. One summer I worked with a combine crew up in Canada."

He looked so much like Charlie. Dell suspected Roy had a lot of family worries on his mind in addition to wanting to find work.

"You realize that you can't talk about my business with anyone."

"I can handle that," he assured his aunt.

"Know anything about planting trees?"

"I can learn."

There were always things that needed fixing, and Jerry could use help planting the shelterbelt at the country place.

Roy helped around the hotel in the evenings by emptying ashtrays, picking up after guests, and generally being available when needed. He grinned as he watched his aunt accept a "drink" from a customer, knowing it was only iced tea served from her special whiskey bottle.

That Lusk was moving away from its frontier status toward modern living was indicated by stories carried in *The Lusk Herald*. New businesses opened; new products appeared. It was a time of excitement. Roy ran into the hotel one day, exclaiming, "Have you seen that new Chrysler Airflow car the Snyders are raffling off? It's a beauty. What I could do with one of those!"

"I don't think so, Roy. They take a lot of gasoline." Dell knew her nephew's finances could not maintain one.

"Well, look at you," he said. "You run around in that Packard of yours all the time." Mischievously, he added, "Looks exactly like Jerry's, too."

"Go on with you." Dell laughed at him. That boy was too much. It was good to have him there.

When Roy became restless in Lusk, Dell sent him to visit his Uncle Herbert in Seattle. After six weeks, Roy was ready to return to Michigan. Roy's exciting summer trip set a precedent for the visits he and Dell enjoyed through the years.

New Year's 1933 did not bring much relief for the depressed economy. The state's oil output had dropped to about one-fourth what it had been in the boom days thirteen to fifteen years earlier. The drought laid siege from Canada to Texas, bringing dust storms that endangered the breathing and lives of animals and humans alike. Nevertheless, February 20 was a day of celebration at the Yellow Hotel. The U.S. Congress passed the 21st Amendment, called the Blaine resolution, to repeal Amendment 18. Prohibition was over.

"Does this mean we get liquor on the house tonight?" asked one of the regulars.

"No, but it does mean that nobody's going to turn me in for selling it or haul you off for drinking it." Dell poured him another drink.

"I can't believe this is the end of Prohibition," another man chimed in. "We been in business so long, it won't seem like home if the still ain't running."

"I can always use good liquor," Dell assured him. "The end of Prohibition just means it'll be legal to make it and sell it." Dell's smile was broader than anyone had seen in a long time.

She shook her auburn curls back in place and set the Mills Studio jukebox to play, "The Best Things in Life Are Free."

The evening went fine until the oil-field crew walked in, already full of whiskey. A tall boy pulled off his wooly cap, revealing blond hair sticking out in all directions. "Hey, want to dance with me?" he yelled at the first girl who walked by.

The girl nodded graciously and moved to join him. When a short dark-haired man grabbed her wrist, Dell knew trouble was brewing. She stepped up to the two men, who were yelling insults. "If you boys want to fight, you'll have to go outside."

"We been down at the Merrywhirl and they was too tame." The blonde almost fell over as he looked down at Dell. "We couldn't get no action over there." He turned to the dark-haired man. "Wanna fight 'bout this?"

"Nah, I just wanna dance. Ya got a problem with that?" The girl tried to pull her wrist out of his grasp and the dark-haired man grabbed her to his chest. "Let's dance."

Without warning, the blond boy lashed out. The dark-haired man's head hit the floor hard from the blow that almost knocked over the girl beside him.

Dell reached for the phone. "Sheriff, we have a problem." He was on his way.

The presidential election of Franklin Delano Roosevelt brought in the New Deal on March 4, 1933, along with the passage of a bill to keep money in government-inspected banks. As people began to return their money to the nation's banks, the economy began a slow upturn.

With the repeal of Prohibition came an easing of the economy, but not enough to relieve the Depression from Lusk. Although she later told Los Angeles newspaper reporter Charles Hillinger that "Prohibition didn't make a dent," Dell's records included days when she took in only a few dollars. She usually took in cash only, recorded without names in her books.

Because Dell isolated herself from most people, her Pekingese dogs became friends who provided unconditional love. In addition, they had become her "signature" in the community as she introduced new girls by having them walk or carry the dogs while shopping downtown.

Her dogs were like children to her. In late March 1933, her beloved Chen Chen died, and she faced the decision whether to replace him or not. Later she would, but not right away. Customers as well as her girls missed the little dog, whose loving attention had been welcome.

While the girls were not allowed to flaunt themselves on the streets of Lusk, Dell did take them to the XL Café some evenings for dinner out. The short walk from the Yellow Hotel gave them a brief but welcome outing. Another regular outing came when Dell took her girls to see Doc Reckling for their monthly checkup. Generally, they were clean, and there were no problems.

On one visit the doctor was in especially good spirits. He had finally received authorization to purchase a new X-ray machine for the Lusk Hospital. "This will help improve my services considerably," he jubilantly told Dell. Technological advances were indeed coming to Lusk.

The droughts of the mid-1930s brought wide swings in weather, from blizzards and record-breaking rainstorms to tornadoes and damaging high winds. All combined to make life on the western prairies difficult in an already unsteady economy. For several years a grasshopper invasion disrupted life as they ate their way across the region, devouring all vegetation, along with clothing drying in the sunshine on outdoor lines. Even fence posts and animals could be targets for the hungry insects. People stayed inside when they could, still having to fight the few hoppers that found a hole to squeeze through.

In 1934 and 1936, the federal government established relief programs to aid the cattlemen. If a rancher didn't have feed, his cattle were shot, butchered, and given to needy families or transported to out-of-state pastures rather than starving. Wild animals foraged for food wherever possible. As farmers' potato crops became ready for harvest, antelope often got there first. The flooded oil market of the early 1930s was not alleviated until the middle of that decade when new markets opened. Next came advancements in geophysics and improved drilling methods. Production doubled.

Everyone was aware of the damage being done by the drought. Dell shopped at the local stores most of the time for groceries and other personal items. A local minister worked at the Safeway grocery store because his church couldn't pay him enough to live on.

Dell stepped up to him. "You pray for a lot of things, don't you?"

A little surprised, he answered, "Yes."

She said, "Well, why don't you pray for these ranchers to get rain? Pray for something good for a change. They really do need rain." Observers wondered whether Dell was worried about the effects of the drought or was having fun with the minister.

A federal program was put in place across the nation to provide food for families without employment. In Lusk Attorney Fagan's widow took the job of distributing prunes, canned meat, and other necessities. At the same time a number of self-sufficient independent families chose to endure these years without seeking aid.

"You know, this whole thing about our ranchers having a hard time puts me in the mind of those years my brother-in-law and me come out here after the war in 'bout 1918 and put in our homestead up in the Hat Creek area." Jerry turned to Dell as he spoke. "Did I ever tell you 'bout that?"

"No, I just knew you homesteaded up there," she replied.

"It wasn't an easy time, and we had to give it up." Jerry sighed. "Then, later, Duff and me heard there was a good market for flax so we put in a crop. Did well, too, for a time. But like now, the market was a roller coaster and we ended up losing it all the next year."

Plans were going forward for Jerry and Maynard Bishop to open bar beside the billiard parlor Maynard already operated in the new Ranger Hotel. Balls were already clicking on the billiard table as players made their shots when Jerry and Dell discussed the idea one night.

"We still don't know for sure we can legally open up a bar. And it'll be right on Main Street."

"Wyoming is going to pass a state resolution to let bars serve liquor," Dell assured Jerry. "It's coming, I know it is."

"How do you know that?"

"I know a lot of people around this state and some of them are in the legislature, remember?"

Jerry glanced at her. "How come you're so sure you want to go in on this?"

"You know this kind of work. You can do it and you know the guys around here. I'm willing to put up your half of the money and you do the work." She knew his pride was wounded. "Pay me off when the money comes in."

"Well, if you're so sure, I'll tell Maynard we can go ahead." Jerry shifted uneasily.

"The billiard parlor's already open. Advertise that even if the bar can't serve liquor." Dell was sure her investment in Jerry as a partner in this business venture and in her life would pay off. He had been dry for a while and seemed to be keeping his life in better order. She hoped that a job would be the rest of the answer.

In April the *Lusk Herald* announced that the Oasis Bar and Club Billiard Parlor in the Ranger Building were open for business, naming Maynard Bishop and Jerry Dull as owners. As she walked through the bar just before it opened, Dell stopped to admire the picture on the back bar in the Oasis. Lightly clad, the buxom woman lounged appealingly against a set of colorful plush pillows on a long sofa.

"That'll give the guys something to look at while they're downing drinks." Maynard winked at her. Billiard tables and equipment were laid out carefully, waiting for customers the next day. The back room, with its slot machines and poker table, was shrewdly placed out of direct view. They were ready.

The drought broke in the spring with a thirty-day rain. It raised spirits as well as grass on the prairies. Despite the flooding that occurred, even calving seemed to go easier with more moisture. Another boom in the oil business brought oil workers back into the county. Money again flowed freely, and the local economy picked up once more.

Oil companies employed roughnecks—a rough and tumble group—to work in the fields. They drank heavily, were lusty, and fought anything fightable, including each other—prime customers for the Yellow Hotel as long as they behaved themselves. Most of them did. This was also the year Wyoming officials passed laws to legalize the sale of hard liquor in addition to the sale of beer.

In 1935 the drowning death of eighteen-year-old Dolores Fisher, Dell's niece (Charlie and Nora's daughter), came as a complete shock. She had been at a lake in Michigan. Once more the sudden loss of a member of her family raised Dell's awareness of how precious the personal relationships in her life really were.

A fully functioning brothel within the Lusk city limits was a contentious issue for the city council. Many people were concerned that Dell might close down the town's lights if they tried to close down her business after she floated a loan to help them rebuild their power plant. Even so, there were still Luskites who felt that the Yellow Hotel was a blot on their landscape. A few went so far as to mention it to her. In response, she was quoted as saying, "If you try to shut me down, I'll shut down the power plant."

For obvious reasons, they couldn't permit that, so the city council reorganized the city limits to put her hotel outside them. Since it was no longer within the city limits, they didn't have to do anything about running her out of town. It was during this time also that it became evident that Dell had financed the operations of many ranchers during the tough times, and they, too, opposed closing her down.

By the late 1930s, Dell was a frequent visitor at the Dull household. One afternoon Dell and Jerry sat talking after lunch.

"Business has been good," Dell commented.

"Yeah, we've both done all right this year."

"Winter's always a slack time at the hotel; let's go somewhere."

"Like Las Vegas?"

"Nah, how about California? I've heard of this really nice place . . . and the weather's warmer there."

"Okay. Why not?"

Thus began annual trips to places where a man and a woman

who loved each other could find privacy.

Housing and business construction reflected the nation's new expansion. The first paved road between Lusk and Lance Creek was completed in 1932. *The Lusk Herald* noted that a modern swimming pool was put in place in 1936, and Main Street parking was changed to diagonal to provide additional spaces. The city of Lusk instituted free garbage and ash collection, requiring that these be placed in covered metal containers in the alleys for pickup.

Repair work, newspaper delivery, and milk routes were among the positions that brought people into contact with Dell. Mike Kilmer was glad to have the milk route, even though work began at 5:00 a.m.

"You just like your job 'cause where it takes you," some of his co-workers teased.

"Dell Burke treats me good, pays her bills on time, gives me no trouble," Mike retorted.

"So what does a madam order from the dairy? Whipped cream?"

"The usual things—milk, butter, and eggs."

"Yeah, and you trade out services with her." The guys were laughing.

"Nah." He shrugged. "She's like anyone else. I deliver to the back door. First of the month I leave her bill in the milk box. Next morning, the money's on the kitchen table. Never see the girls."

One highlight of 1938 for Dell was the opportunity to purchase two more lots that adjoined her hotel on First Street. Mabel Hassed decided to let them go and in mid-August the transaction was completed. Now Dell owned almost the entire block.

However, she chose to erect no new buildings on the now vacant lots. With these purchases, she invested in real estate, invested in the town of Lusk, and secured more privacy for her operations.

Jerry's creativity and electrical know-how sometimes combined with his sense of humor in the pool hall. He was well-liked and easy to talk with. Along one wall, spectators sat on a bench or chairs. Jerry wired one particular chair with a button underneath that could be pressed to give the guys on the bench a shock. For a lark, one day he rewired it so that when the button was pressed, the person sitting in the chair rather than those on the bench got the shock. One of the regulars, Forrest Van Tassel, came in and sat in the chair.

Soon, Forrest grinned, leaned forward to press the button, and got a surprise. Instead of someone on the bench letting out a yelp, Forrest got zapped.

Through the window in the front door, Dell saw Mr. O'Connor walking along the sidewalk toward her. Before she could get the door open, Dell saw his car slowly begin to roll down the sloping driveway toward the street.

Horrified, she threw open the door and hurried out. Two children's faces were pressed against the windows as their dad raced back to stop the car before it went into the street. As Mr. O'Connor reached the car, money flew out of his hand.

"Whew! That was close," he exclaimed.

"Are the kids all right?"

"Yeah, scared; but they're okay."

"I'm so glad—that was frightening."

Dell helped him pick up the dollar bills fluttering around on the ground. "You're always right on time with your payments."

"I'm sure grateful you backed my loan. Don't know what we'd have done without you."

In 1939 Roy Fisher, his wife, Phyllis, and her mother, were overnight guests at the Yellow Hotel. Roy quietly noted that none of the girls were in evidence.

It was a special visit for them all. "I've been wanting to show Phyllis your place and the West," Roy told his Aunt Marie. She had been looking forward to meeting his new wife, too. It had been about six years since Roy had worked for her and Jerry, but they both remembered that time fondly.

"Want to see the country place where Roy helped plant trees? I'd have you stay out there, but it's too small for visitors, and I'm still fixing it up."

Over dinner that night, Roy asked, "Did you know they called this decade the 'Dirty Thirties'?"

"Was that because of the drought and dust bowl conditions?"

"Yeah, I guess there was so much dirt flying around someone decided that fit."

"It certainly did," Marie agreed. Jerry just grinned.

WAR YEARS AND RECOVERY, 1940–1949

The oil booms of earlier years were fading, and new prospects were not yet obvious. The hotel rode out the quietus as a lull between waves of activity. Population in Lusk dwindled to 1,814 while Niobrara County contained fewer than six thousand residents. A worldwide alarm had been sounded when Germany invaded Poland in late 1939. Unrest in Europe threatened international peace.

While the international scene seemed distant, the draft was beginning to draw young men from the rural west. Tension was building among the young men who expected to enlist if that was required.

A game at the Oasis Bar and Club Billiards Parlor provided an opportunity to consider the possibilities.

"Wonder what's goin' to happen."

"I think there'll be a war."

"Aw, I don't think it'll go that far."

"I do, and if we go to war, I'm going. I don't want none of them people coming over here telling us how to run our country."

The pros and cons of war and the results of entering the military were considered; then the issue of whether that next ball would hit the corner pocket became a pressing point that consumed the attention and energy at the table.

While the men played billiards, Dell was taking one of her occasional four- to five-block walks to see the Smiths, which she saw as a good opportunity for a little exercise and good companionship. Dell enjoyed conversation over a cup of coffee with Bill and Hester Smith.

"You know, Bill, even after all these years, people still look down on me because of my business," Dell began, "but if it wasn't for me, there wouldn't be any lights here now."

"You've done this town more good than it'll ever know."

"But I don't think they can see me for the hotel business. It's like Dell Burke and the hotel business are the same thing. Both dirty."

"That's gotta be tough."

Dell sipped her coffee pensively. "At the same time," she said thoughtfully, "it's handy that so many folks know me. Out-of-towners stop at the bars, restaurants, and gas stations . . . everyone knows where the Yellow Hotel is, so . . . it's easy to get directions."

Bill grinned and reached for another cup of coffee.

Business at Club Billiards and the Oasis had been running smoothly for several years, but that partnership was brought to an end with the death of Maynard Bishop in 1941.

"What are you going to do now?" Dell asked Jerry.

"Not sure. His wife might take over Maynard's end."

Soon, it was decided. Bessie Bishop would remain in business as Jerry's partner with help from her daughter, Leta, and Jerry would continue to manage the billiards end. A bartender would have to be hired for the Oasis.

"Who'll tend bar?" Dell asked. "You shouldn't do that."

"I know and I've been talking with Eddie Plumb. He just got to Lusk and needs a job. He seems to be a nice feller. His wife's Opal, and she's a hard worker. She comes from around Lusk, so he'll probably stick around."

Dell nodded. Eddie was a good choice.

Newcomers to Lusk were often curious about the good-looking woman who carried a dog as she shopped. Ray Taylor had not been in town long before he found a job at the Midwest Hardware store. "Who's that nice lady with the little dog?" he asked his boss, Harry Fernau Sr., of the small, attractive, auburn-haired woman who was always well dressed, wore a stylish hat, and carried a small Pekingese dog.

"That's Dell Burke."

Ray walked over to her. "May I help you?"

Dell smiled. "I need a new washing machine." She considered several before choosing a Maytag.

Ray delivered the wringer-type machine to the laundry room at the back of the hotel.

Even though they had shared interesting conversation over the washing machine purchase, Ray noticed that the next time he saw her on the street, she nodded and did not speak. When he asked Harry why she wouldn't talk to him, he learned that while Dell enjoyed visiting with salespeople, she usually maintained a discreet distance on the street to avoid any embarrassment for her or them.

During the long years of Prohibition some men learned to numb their lives with alcohol, and after it was over, some found it hard to stop drinking. When a teenager named Mike picked up his uncle, drunk and crying between trips to vomit in the bathroom at the Oasis Bar, Jerry had a tonic.

To the young man's surprise, Jerry handed him a quart of whiskey and advised him to give his uncle a nip whenever he needed it to keep him quiet for the three-hour drive to Hot Springs.

Jerry helped Mike load his six-foot-tall uncle into the car. "Don't tell him you're taking him to dry out or he'll jump out, sure thing."

On December 7, 1941, Japan attacked U.S. forces in Pearl Harbor. The United States declared war on Japan the following day. The waiting was over, and soon many of Lusk's young men left to enlist.

Although the war took many of the young men away from the area, others came through on troop trains or from nearby military bases. In addition, the war required increased fuel supplies, which revived oil production.

"It's an ill wind that brings no one good," Jerry commented wryly.

"I'm sorry it's war that brings our economy back to life," Dell replied. The upswing in the oil business had brought a surge of new life to the state and community.

"They've been looking for new oil the last several years. Lance Creek's booming again."

"It's good for both of our businesses." She smiled.

Jerry shook his head. "We've already begun to lose men over there."

"But the ones coming through on the trains sure help business." Dell brightened. It was already becoming a prosperous year. "That new air base west of Casper is bringing us customers."

"Yeah, even though the military thinks the base is too far from us to make a difference, the men still drive the hundred miles to Lusk."

With the increased business, the hotel's future was stable once more. Dell decided it was time to take possession of all her lands in Lusk. On February 13, 1942, Francis Day, who had assumed paper liability for the small house in 1932, signed it back over to Dell.

The war years made many differences in the daily lives of Luskites. Victory gardens produced homegrown vegetables for households already conservation conscious. Gasoline and rubber rationing decreased automobile travel. Sugar, flour, and other staples were in short supply, as were shoes, coats, and material for new clothes.

Lusk's proximity to Ft. Warren Air Force Base in Cheyenne, Casper's new military operation, and the railroad made it inviting to lonesome soldiers, sailors, and marines, who appreciated the honky-tonk atmosphere of the Yellow Hotel and nearby bars.

In addition to bringing customers to the hotel, the operations of nearby military facilities sometimes brought unexpected excitement. One morning the clock by Dell's bed said it was much too early to get up, but she recognized the sheriff's voice at once when she picked up the ringing phone. "Hey, Dell, did you know you have company out at your country place?"

"What's going on?"

"I think you'll want to come out." It sounded urgent. "Seven men were on their first training mission out of the Casper airbase and their B-17 ran out of gas."

"Anyone hurt?" Suddenly, she was wide-awake.

"Nah, not really. They're shook up a bit. Had to make a forced landing but they bailed out in time. One landed in your pasture, and another one over near Pete Owen's ranch."

It was always something. Dell had her hands full. Not only were military personnel crowding her rooms, but the oil business also brought hordes of rough-as-a-cob workers fresh from the field. Keeping the customers in line was almost a full-time job.

The business-transaction procedure at the Yellow Hotel was the same each time. The man approached the door—front if he was a newcomer or out-of-towner or the back if he was a regular. Dell met him at the door and took him into a waiting room, where she quickly assessed whether he was drunk. If he was, she simply asked him to leave. If he refused, she called the sheriff. If the man passed inspection, he was offered a drink and an opportunity to meet girls. When he chose one, they went upstairs to a bedroom, where there was an iron-frame single bed beside a washstand. The basin and water pot were used for inspecting the man's private parts for disease prior to actual services. A special clocklike timer downstairs notified the girls, their customers, and Dell when the time was up.

Sometimes Dell's girls got out of hand. Too much drinking or dancing with another girl's man could lead to a hair-pulling squabble. When that happened, Dell called Sheriff Del Shoopman. "Come get 'em. They're at each other and they won't stop."

The sheriff took the girls to jail, where they rattled bars and sang loudly. Above the jail, he and his wife ate dinner. Often their granddaughter, Dotty, who lived down the street, ate with them. The commotion was easy to hear from the table. After dinner, Dotty slipped downstairs into the outer room near the jail cell.

"Hi, there," called a girl in a cancan dress. Dotty nodded shyly, observing their fancy jewelry, corsets, makeup, and wonderfully smelling perfume.

"You're a cute little girl. Who are you?"

"I'm Dotty. I was upstairs with my grandma and grandpa."

Another girl asked if she liked to dance. Dotty had been taking tap dance lessons. "I love to."

The girl showed her some dance steps. When Dotty went back upstairs to her grandparent's place, she showed off her new steps.

Her grandma became suspicious. "Why did she give you a tap dance lesson?" she asked.

"She likes Peppermint Patties, so I gave her some." Now Dotty was in trouble.

Over later meals with her grandparents, Dotty learned about Dell Burke. Her grandpa, Lusk's sheriff from 1937 to 1948, had many different interactions with the madam. "Remember that time the mayor wanted to shut down the Yellow Hotel?" he liked to ask his wife. "The City Council was harassing her and she reminded them of the time she went down to shut the city water off. That was when that young feller just out of UW was the town engineer."

"I remember," was the patient answer. This story was often repeated at their table.

"He was in charge of the water program, but he stuttered so hard Dell couldn't understand him. And the more she protested, the more nervous he got and the worse he stuttered. She was mad anyway, but finally he coaxed her into not shutting the water off."

"Was that the time," Mrs. Shoopman asked, "Dell said most of the guys had done business at the hotel, and if they kept bothering her she'd tell their wives?"

"I think it was. Stopped 'em cold."

The sheriff finished his story as he often did. "You know, she's done this town a whole lot of good, and there's a passel of sheepherders out there who owe their lives to her." He paused. "And there's the cowboys who trailed cattle through Lusk she put up and fed. Those were hard times, and they'd have been in real trouble without Dell Burke."

"You know, Dell and Jerry are quite a pair," Mrs. Shoopman said slowly. "Always taking care of somebody down on their luck. Good hearted, they are."

Newsreels that played before the cartoon and main feature in the movie theaters kept viewers aware of the war—and grateful that it was not being fought on American soil. Locals mourned the loss of young people, and when the Germans surrendered to the Allies in May 1945, moviegoers watched gratefully. The war was beginning to end.

The German surrender was discussed throughout town, including in the Oasis Bar and Club Billiards Parlor. Balls were clicking on the billiard table almost as fast as conversation was running above it.

"Did you hear about the Germans, Jerry?"

"It's about time. Ever since we marched into Normandy last year, it's been nip and tuck." He sighted along his cue stick.

"The Japs gotta give in next. Wonder what that'll take." The next player leaned over the table, figuring the angles.

Talk around the pool table turned to the men and women who would not be coming home from the war and hailed the ones who would be home soon. It had been a long haul. Questions about what it might be like without rationing and where they would go on their first long drive out of town raised curiosity.

Less than a month after the United States dropped the first atomic bomb on Japan in August 1945, the Japanese surrendered, and the war ground to a halt. International relationships needed to be renegotiated to establish trade and to provide aid for damaged countryside. Once the war ended, oil business boomed with new vigor. Pipeliners, along with construction and oil-field workers, continued to visit the Yellow Hotel.

On October 26, 1945, Florence A. Brown warranty deeded her country property, including the house, to Dell Burke, concluding the transaction that had begun about fifteen years earlier.

"So, what do you want to do next with the country place?" Jerry asked Dell, sensing that Dell's mind was already at work.

"I'd like to go really modern. Paint the walls green, cover the old fireplace with plaster and paint it pink. Get Lucite furniture. Chrome on the sofa would be real keen."

"Anything else?"

"I'm thinking of remodeling, too. I found someone good with construction work. I'll call him and see what he can do."

Soon after, Dell told Duff Hollon's son, Jerry, "Here's how I want it to look." They settled on a starting time, and he picked up supplies. She gave clear instructions for what she wanted done and wrote it down or drew diagrams of the work. Dell always paid promptly and was courteous to work with, and Jerry Hollon liked working with her. While there were men in the community who shied away from working for Dell, others found her to be a good employer. Whether they were putting up hay, doing carpentry, doing repairs, or working on odd jobs, they appreciated her fairness and honesty.

Eddie Plumb tended bar at the Oasis for several years after Maynard Bishop died. Eddie and his wife, Opal, became friendly with Jerry and Dell. Jerry was excited about changes they were making at the country property, and he wanted to show off the trees and bushes he had planted near the house.

"Hey, Eddie, want to go out and see what we're doing out there?"

"Sure. Opal's coming by shortly. How about taking her with us?"

And so the Plumbs got a sneak peek at the renovations and new paint job. Later, Dell invited them out for a steak fry. The large barbecue grill built into the yard wall made meal preparation easy.

The country place provided privacy for dignitaries who wanted to dine, drink, play cards, and relax with feminine companionship or just spend an evening of quiet political scheming. It was also where Dell and Jerry found precious time away from curious eyes and where the girls enjoyed leisure away from the hotel.

The Yellow Hotel provided a safe sexual outlet for its customers due to the regular medical inspections that Dell insisted on for her girls. Although numerous people observed the women at the doctor's office for their health inspections, some visits were made in the privacy of the hotel. Mildred Pinkerton learned this firsthand one day. Just out of high school, Mildred worked as nurse's aide for Doc Reckling, who was the Niobrara County health inspector. One afternoon Doc pulled out his bag, looked over the needles, syringes, and equipment, and put it all together. With bag in hand, he turned to Mildred and said, "I'm going over to the Yellow Hotel to inspect the girls. I need you to come along." Mildred blushed, pulled on a jacket, and climbed in the car. She held the equipment until they reached the hotel, then she scrunched down to wait in the car until he was through.

Another day Nurse Ruby Brown was pressed into service to accompany the doctor on his rounds at the hotel. "I'm not sure if I want people to know that sometimes I work at the Yellow Hotel," she protested. Doc glanced at her over the top of his small, wire-rimmed glasses and snorted.

Bob Vollmer occasionally assumed chauffeur duty for Doc Reckling after his discharge from the army in 1945. Doc would indicate the hotel's front door and tell Bob, "Pull up right here. That's the closest way to carry things in." Doc didn't allow hesitation, nor did he consider discretion. At other times, Bob was called on to transport the doctor to the hotel on emergency runs. When the girls got sick, Doc Reckling often asked Bob to drive him to the hotel.

"Where you going?" his friends would ask.

Bob's answer, "Down to see Dell and party," became a standing joke. Bob usually sat and visited with Dell while Doc tended the girls. One night while they talked, Dell was called away to the telephone. While she was gone, one of the girls wandered into the room. Attractively made up and prettily dressed, she sauntered over and sat down beside Bob. Before they could move beyond casual conversation, Dell came back.

"What are you doing down here?" Dell demanded. "Get back upstairs. This is one of my personal friends." Her voice grew louder with each word. "Don't you dare come around him again." The girl left immediately. Dell was protective of men who were friends and would not become customers.

Eventually Bob went to work full-time for Jerry at Club Billiards. While it was evident that Jerry had drunk heavily in earlier years, Bob never saw him take a drink on the job.

But temptation did get the better of Jerry at times. More than once he could not seem to stop drinking, and he stayed home drunk until Dell found someone to take him to the alcohol treatment center in Hot Springs, South Dakota, where he'd "dry out" again.

One day Jerry returned from one of those trips quite inebriated. "What happened?" Dell demanded.

"Well, he insisted we stop at every bar on the way back," was the sheepish answer.

"Boy, that did a lot of good!"

But Jerry was back home and stayed dry. For a while.

Dell still grieved for her favorite brother, Charlie, and it was almost as great a loss to Dell when she learned in 1946 that his wife, Nora, had died. Nora had been so close to Dell, so much help in the 1930s, and the only person Dell totally trusted. "I will stay in touch with all the children," Dell vowed to herself, a tear trickling down her cheek as she sat quietly in her room pondering this event. "As long as I live, I will stay in touch with them." This was a promise she kept to the best of her ability.

Promoting business in Lusk was uppermost in the minds of many local business people. Doc Reckling had come across a pioneer event that had occurred about ten to fifteen miles south of Lusk, and it sounded like an opportunity to create an outdoor production. He talked about it with everyone he could, including his patients.

"Doc Reckling's been talking about that pageant for the last two years," Dell complained to Jerry one night. "Think he and Eva Lou Bonsell will ever get it together?"

"I think it's a go for next year." Jerry smiled. "From what I hear, the script's done and they're auditioning people for the parts."

Dell was curious about the pageant. *The Legend of Rawhide*

Buttes described a bloody incident where a member of a wagon train shot an Indian maid, and the Indians had attacked the wagon train demanding they be given the shooter. After the shooter was finally turned over to the Indians, he was skinned alive. When Dell and the Doc happened to run into each other in the hospital waiting room, he told her, "I've invented a knife that'll cut through the outer layer of ketchup-filled red underwear Clyde's gonna wear when the Indians skin him." Dell was disgusted. "Coming to see the pageant?" Doc asked.

With her usual diplomacy, Dell replied, "If I can."

But they both knew she would probably not only be busy at the hotel, but also that she stayed away from community events to avoid embarrassing local men and women or herself.

Dell had a good sense of humor. She had to. Her hotel, her girls, her business, and even she herself were humorously targeted by the men, women, and young people of the area. It was not uncommon for jokes to be played on men who worked for her at the hotel or the country place.

One such man was Curly, who did repair work at the hotel. Someone saw him coming out of the hotel and asked, "Hey Curly, how was it?"

"How was what?" Curly replied, then realized what was meant. "Ah, I didn't get any, but I found her electrical problem." He took a lot of ribbing about that.

At Culver & Son plumbing shop, the salesclerks enjoyed having a good laugh. When a new salesman came by, he was told, "Hey, you've got a call."

"Where's that?"

"You're supposed to call so-and-so. The number's . . . "

The number belonged to the Yellow Hotel. Such wrong numbers were not unusual at the hotel.

The new vacuum cleaner salesman was a perfect target for a joke. Several men were drinking coffee at the hardware store as he walked in. The storeowner told the salesman, "There's a lady down at the Yellow Hotel who wants to buy a vacuum cleaner."

Although the salesman did not know the Yellow Hotel, he quickly realized that it was no ordinary hotel. When he returned to the store to have coffee with the guys, they were laughing at the big joke they played on him.

The storeowner asked, "How'd you do?"

"Not too bad for a morning," he said. "She wants one for upstairs and one for downstairs, but she said the only way she'll pay for 'em is if the hardware store manager'll bring them to her when he comes by." Dell was insightful about the jokes about her and her business, and this time the joke had been turned back on the jokers.

In 1948 Matt Cunningham (name changed for anonymity) stepped inside the Yellow Hotel for the first time. He was revisiting his hometown, and he was thirsty. He had heard of the hotel all his life and had decided it was time to find out what it was like.

Dell led him into the main room and asked if he wanted a drink.

Matt glanced around. The room was immaculately clean. Elegant chandeliers provided dusky lighting in the mahogany-paneled room. A comfortable couch covered with velvet flowers held a man he didn't know. Other chairs and another couch offered additional seating, under velvet curtains that were closed for privacy.

"I hear you have good whiskey. How about a shot of that?"

The taste was pleasant, but he was shocked to find it cost $1. He did not speak to the two attractive girls lounging nearby, since companionship was not on his mind that night. But later he got to thinking about them. The slender dark-haired girl with laughter in her eyes had caught his imagination.

When Matt next arrived at the hotel, the jukebox was playing the "Portuguese Washerwoman." The dark-haired girl was occupied, so he chose another one. She was in her early twenties, and an excellent dancer. They glided across the floor with little competition and with considerable grace. It was pleasant to have her in his arms, and he decided to take her upstairs. He made the arrangements with Dell.

"Fees vary from $5 to $10, depending on what you want," she said.

Matt became a regular customer at Dell's Hotel, enjoying conversation with the madam as well as with her girls. When Dell realized Matt and one of the other customers knew each other, she arranged it so they would not meet. Matt had sampled other brothels and could tell that Dell had made hers a safe place where he could drink without fear of getting drunk and being rolled for the rest of his money. Nor was he concerned about going upstairs with a "crazy woman" or about catching a disease from one of them.

Matt visited often but avoided the hotel on weekends when the pipeliners came to town and during hunting season. Matt's story is not an unusual one. Other customers visited Dell's Yellow Hotel under the same circumstances. They found that it was a safe place and that her services—from the alcohol served to the girls who worked there—could be trusted.

Dell believed in keeping her appearance attractive and made

regular trips to beauty parlors and clothing stores. While she often shopped in Lusk, she varied where she spent her money, and she also favored several high-end Denver stores. Ruth Fleming worked as a cosmetologist for one of the beauty shops where Dell had a shampoo and set from time to time. At other times she went to Kut and Kurl, which was run by Evelyn Vollmer.

When either Dell or her girls needed an appointment, Dell generally scheduled visits when the shop was least busy with other patrons to avoid embarrassing either herself or the women who would be there.

One day Faye Baker, who was sitting in a chair while her hair dried, turned to Dell, and inquired, "How're you today?"

"I'm fine, and you?" came Dell's reply.

Using a technique she was adept at, Dell turned the conversation to daily life, asking questions about the cattle and horses on the Baker ranch. The sort of thing most ranchers' wives talked about. Thus she avoided discussing her personal or professional life.

From time to time, Dell upgraded her transportation. "Time to replace my car," she announced one day. "The old one has given good service, but it's time for a change. Besides, the new ones are so pretty!"

She marched down to the Chrysler Garage to look over the new cars. Selecting one she believed would suit her best, she pulled out her purse. With the price set, she began counting out $5 bills to pay for it. The salesman smiled. He had heard that $5 was the going rate at the hotel.

Winter had begun earlier that year, and in November 1948 a blizzard brought flurries that continued to build the snowpack. Shortly after Christmas, another storm arrived, and the snow continued to fall heavily. Winds picked up, and soon blizzard conditions were reached once more. Drifting snow changed the landscape hourly and piled to the rooftops of low-lying buildings. Travel was impossible. For about three days, snow fell and wind blew across the western states from Montana to Texas and from Nebraska to California. The Blizzard of '49 is still remembered throughout the West.

Ranchers often say, "Look out for snowstorms with small flakes. They keep coming down for a long time," and this one did. Even ranchers who wanted to milk their cows did not wander out in such weather; one who did became confused by the drifting snow and froze to death. Many people were snowbound in Lusk. Hotels filled beyond capacity. Snow continued to fall, filling streets, highways, and train tracks.

One place where rooms could be found was the Yellow Hotel, and Dell extended hospitality to any man needing a place to stay. For years Earl Criss had worked across the street from the Yellow Hotel as the station master at the Lusk Depot. The Blizzard of '49 found him stranded in town at the depot along with other railroad engineers and workers. He was relieved to find a place to stay, and the next day, he called his wife, Matilda. "Guess where I stayed last night, Tilly?" When he explained, they shared a good laugh about it, yet both were grateful he had found safe, warm lodging.

The next day some men went back to the depot hoping to leave, but they couldn't, so they called their wives to let them know where they were. When asked where they had stayed, they said only that they had stayed in a hotel, and they did *not* tell which one.

After the night at the Yellow Hotel, one man could not find his billfold. Dell found him in a quandary and asked, "Did you lose this?"

In her hand was his billfold. "It was lying around, and I put it in my lockbox for safekeeping."

When the blizzard finally stopped, the beautiful clear blue sky exposed huge snowdrifts that glistened blindingly in bright sunshine. Tunnels began to appear as people worked their way toward stores and between homes. It would be weeks before the snow removal system could adequately clear railroad tracks for passage. Winter was not over, and snow fell throughout the spring months before finally stopping in April.

As life returned to its normal routine, Dell was reminded that her Pekingese had a mind of his own. The hotel was fine, but he liked to explore. "He's been gone for over an hour," Dell fretted to one of her girls who was standing beside her at the back door. Despite their efforts the dog could not be found and did not come home. Two days passed, and he still did not appear. The girl went looking again. A short way up the hill above the hotel, she noticed a young boy in the doorway of the Bonners' house. She stopped and asked him, "Have you seen a small cuddly brown dog running about?"

Butch Bonner nodded. "Is it yours?"

"It might be."

Butch went inside and brought out the Pekingese.

"Oh, thank you." The girl hugged the dog with relief. Young Butch nodded sadly. He had hoped no one would come for the cute little dog.

Shopping trips in town offered Dell an opportunity to visit with friends as well as to pick up supplies. Dell had several stops planned that blustery spring day in the late 1940s as she parked her car on Main Street. It would help to have the car conveniently nearby so she could load it with packages.

Her first stop was at *The Lusk Herald* for a cup of coffee and conversation with Editor Jim Griffith. He was always full of news and had become a good friend. When Dell asked the girl at the counter, "Where's that Jim?" she pointed at the editor's office with a smile.

At Coast to Coast Hardware, Dell looked along the shelves for a new alarm clock. Her dog had knocked the old one on the floor. "May I help you?" asked the petite salesgirl, who was called Tiny.

After Dell left, Tiny's husband, Lawrence, asked if she knew who her customer had been. "I only know that she is one of the pleasantest people to wait on. She's very quiet and she never pushes in anywhere." Tiny was surprised to learn one of her favorite customers was *the* Dell Burke.

Dressed in a turquoise winter coat with a fur collar and one of her favorite hats, Dell pushed a cart along the aisle toward the bakery counter where Bess Ruffing worked. "What can I do for you today?" Bess asked.

"A loaf of your good French bread would be nice. Any fresh baked today?"

"Made it this morning. One loaf?" Bess looked at Dell, thinking, "You'd never know what she does for a living just looking at her. She's so neat and tidy—looks like the rest of us."

"Yes, thanks." Dell added the bread to her cart and continued her shopping.

The last stop was at a home where the lady sold art supplies. One of her girls wanted to paint a picture. Marie Willson was in the living room with her preteen daughter looking for paint to use on art plaster plaques she made. Mary Jean looked across the room at the small, attractive lady in a dark dress. She glanced at her mother and realized that she was hurrying to complete her purchase and leave. Suddenly, Mary Jean realized who this lady was. As they drove away past the street leading to the Yellow Hotel, her mother said abruptly, "You kids stay away from that place."

Dell and the Yellow Hotel affected Luskites one way or the other. Some avoided her, and others were curious about the discreet attractive lady who held herself at a distance with quiet dignity. Always well-dressed, wearing modest makeup and good clothing, Dell and the girls stood out from the windblown, suntanned locals. Discretion was still a key word at the Yellow Hotel, but Dell had begun to relax the rules a bit. The girls were allowed to don swimsuits or brief apparel for a sunbathing excursion into the backyard at the hotel on sunny days. They were behind a tall fence, but they still did not fully escape the curious eyes.

Later that spring, she received a phone call from Michigan that brought excitement and pleasure, but it also raised concerns for her family.

"Aunt Marie," Roy began, "the doctor told us to take Loraine west to recuperate in a drier climate for a couple months."

"What's wrong with her?" her great-aunt demanded anxiously.

"She's been pretty sick with tuberculosis and we've found a place in Colorado where we can stay a while. We thought we'd stop and see you on the way back."

"I'm so sorry to hear she's been sick. Of course, I'd love to have you stop here and visit. Any idea when that'll be?"

"We'll call you when the time gets closer."

Business would be put on hold while they were there, but it would be wonderful to have them visit. Two months later, the next call came. Marie told the family, "Meet me here at the hotel, and we'll all go out to the country place for a visit. I haven't had a chance to show you the bushes we put in or the painting I did this spring."

It was a short visit, but one which impressed Loraine, the great-niece. As they prepared to leave, the seven-year-old said, "Aunt Marie, I'd like to write to you."

Marie was delighted, and thus began their years of correspondence.

Sunday afternoon at the country place was a good time to sit back and relax. The horses and cats had been fed, and the dog had been bathed.

Jerry began to look back over the year. "We give to a lot of local events and charities. Wouldn't it be neat if we could somehow count it on our income tax?"

"To offset some of our income?" Dell asked. That sounded like a good idea. As part of her legal maneuvering, Dell had realized it would be wise to pay federal taxes on the operations of the hotel.

"Yeah. We both helped Mike Kilmer get equipment for his softball team. What else?"

"It was fun becoming a charter member of the Lusk Country Club." Dell laughed.

"Wonder what they'd do if you showed up out there for one of their meetings?" Jerry smiled.

"Won't find out." As always, Dell was adamant about that.

Jerry grinned. "I know. You've always been discreet."

Dell was very comfortable providing financial support for many local projects, but she carefully avoided attending most public events. This may have been due to her desire to protect her customers, or it may have been related to discomfort or shame about her profession. It probably made it easier to maintain the privacy of her double life.

A Frontier Town Grows Up,
1950–1959

Lusk's economy was good as the 1950s arrived, and its population rose to more than two thousand. Lance Creek oil fields were going strong and, along with the construction of Rural Electrification Act lines, brought in many new faces. Ranching was an active industry in the surrounding county, and Main Street businesses expanded.

On June 25, 1950, President Harry S. Truman addressed the nation: Russia had invaded Korea, and North Korea embraced communism while South Korea held out for democracy. The following day, the Korean War began and lasted until 1953. As usual, military action meant business for the Yellow Hotel.

Prostitution had never been legalized in the state, and Wyoming voted to make it illegal in the early 1950s. The governor of Wyoming called the state's sheriffs to Cheyenne to tell them to end brothel action statewide. On his return to Lusk, Sheriff Sam Thomas met with Dell Burke. "I'm sorry to have to tell you this, but the governor wants us to close down all prostitution in the state. That includes your hotel."

Dell was quiet for a moment before replying, "If I have to close the hotel, I'll have to close down the light plant." The discussion continued, but the brothel in Lusk was never closed down.

When Flora and Les Huff brought their airline business to Lusk in October 1949, they had no idea what role their quiet country neighbor would play in their lives. The Huffs had two young daughters ill with cerebral palsy when they moved into a house without electricity or running water east of Dell's country place. In addition, start-up time for new businesses is generally at least two years, and the Huff Air Transportation system was not unusual.

Their neighbor took advantage of the air transportation service Les offered. Dell found it convenient for trips to Denver and Salt Lake to purchase supplies and occasionally just to get away from Lusk. Huff's services carried her girls regularly to Denver, Salt Lake, and other destinations.

Flora occasionally talked with the girls and found them much like the other women she met in Lusk. Dell's small country place was down the road from the airport, and each time Flora took a child to the doctor or went for groceries, she drove past it. She noticed a man there, and assumed he and Dell were a ranching couple like other neighbors. After a year or so passed, Flora realized that this neighbor's business had made it possible for the Huffs to pay for groceries, medical treatment, and supplies. Without that early patronage, the Huffs would have had a difficult time.

Flora was grateful. "Honey," she told Les, "I'm going to bake cookies and take them over to Dell to show her how much I appreciate her."

Les paused. "I don't think you should do that, Flora." Dell had asked him not to discuss her business with anyone, but now he needed to explain it to his wife. Flora was aghast. A good Christian woman with rather "straight-laced" values, she found it hard to reconcile the kindness Dell had shown with the profession she practiced.

"But you know," she told Les, "the Bible tells us not to judge people, and I respect Dell for what she's done for us. Without her help, we would not have survived those first couple of years."

After Flora had come to terms with Dell's profession, she told her neighbor, "You know, I appreciate what you did for us."

Dell answered firmly, "Mrs. Huff, please do not speak to me in public because I do not want to embarrass you or myself."

So Flora never did. But when they met one on one, Dell always spoke to her. It was with great gratitude that Flora told Les, "You know she asked nothing in return."

Sometimes Dell rode the plane to Denver by herself and then boarded another plane for somewhere else. On one such trip, Les's curiosity got the better of him. "Dell, what do you do when you take these flights? Do you work?"

"Oh well, Mr. Huff," Dell answered, "when I'm on vacation, I'm on vacation."

Needless to say, Les did not ask further.

As the airline business became successful, Dell reduced her usage. After the Huffs were able to obtain electricity and water for their home and the business prospered, Dell stopped calling on them. She knew they didn't need her anymore. Dell believed in supporting local businesses and helping when she saw people in need. Her generosity was often quietly but effectively provided.

It was rotation time again and a new girl had just arrived. When Lotty came in from Salt Lake City, there was excitement at the Yellow Hotel. How would this lanky blonde fit in? Who would be her friends? The other girls liked to sit in on that first meeting Dell held with a new girl. Cup of coffee in hand, the petite auburn-haired madam began listing the rules.

"You'll notice that we dress attractively, but we don't flaunt our bodies in public. Apply your makeup modestly. No gaudy jewelry. Perfume is okay." Dell glanced at the girl's hair. "We have several beauty shops in town. When you want your hair or nails done, let me know and I'll make an appointment."

Lotty sipped her coffee.

"*Never* speak to customers on the street. Don't even look at them if they're with a woman, and don't speak to women out there, either."

With eyebrows knit over half-closed eyes, Lotty asked, "So, we do get to leave the hotel?"

"We go out for dinner occasionally. We spend most Sundays at my country place. No work that day. Here at the hotel, you can sit in the backyard under the umbrella table to read or drink a soda or whatever when you aren't working. No nude sunbathing."

"Not too different from other houses where I've worked."

"Tomorrow, we'll go for the mail and I'll show you Main Street. You can walk my little dog."

The girl laughed and wrinkled her nose. "Why your dog?"

"Folks know that means you work here."

Dell's demeanor was stern as she continued. "My girls drink tea while they're working. They don't get in fights over men or anything else. Come to me and we'll talk it out."

The saucy blonde grinned. "What happens if someone gets unruly?" One of the other girls winked at her.

"She's out of here the next day. I won't allow fighting, drunken behavior, or rough stuff from either my girls or our customers." Dell went on, "One more thing. Doc Reckling will give you a physical exam each month. If you don't come up clean, exams'll be weekly until you are." She added, " And speaking of clean—I don't know what they taught you at other houses, but I want you to inspect every man who goes upstairs with you. There's a pitcher and basin on the nightstand with water, soap, and clean towels. Use them. Every time. Check him over for sores and make sure he gets fun out of it, too."

Lotty glanced around the room. It was clean, neat, and furnished much like any good country home living room, with sofas and chairs around the sides. A lamp stood at one end, and a jukebox was ready to supply music. The bar was clean with glasses that sparkled. She nodded. "I'll like working here though the rooms up there are kinda bare."

"Most men come for one thing, and they don't care about frills like you have in Deadwood or Denver houses," Dell replied. "They don't want 'em. We don't have 'em. Solid plain iron beds, a chenille bedspread over clean sheets—that's all they ask. For most jobs, the fee is $10, which I collect before you go upstairs. I split that with you later on. Did you see the clock on your way in here?"

"Sure is a strange looking thing."

"But it's very effective, and it keeps us all on time." Dell was emphatic. She looked at the new girl closely as she said, "One more thing. You'll be here about two months and you'll rotate out to a place in the Black Hills, then you'll be back here. We have an agreement with houses in several other towns around here to switch the girls from time to time."

"Why rotate us so soon?" Lotty wondered.

"Keeps you from falling in love with our local guys and provides variety for customers. Now, get acquainted with the other girls, and if anyone needs me, I'll be in my apartment. Okay?"

Heads nodded as Dell left cradling her small dog in her arms. The girls gathered around the newcomer.

"Where you from?"

"You won't be sorry you came here."

"Yeah, I've heard about this place. Lots quieter than the West Coast. This is like vacation!" The blonde leaned back.

"She has rules. You know, one time this girl left the hotel, went to a bar, and ran into a truck driver. They got liquored up and went down to Lingle, where they kept drinking and tore up a cafe. When the gal came back, Dell had her suitcase packed, drove her over to the Ranger Hotel, and put her on the next bus that came in. Dell waited with the girl until she was on the bus."

"Then there was the time a couple of girls decided to go play and headed to the Buckaroo. When Dell heard about it, she called the sheriff, and he picked them up out east walking along the road. She sent them off the next day."

"Another time, one girl went downtown to the bars and tried to pick up guys. When Dell found out, she sent her packing right away."

A girl with long brown hair leaned forward. "Not all of us get in trouble. Some learn a lot here and take it with us. Like that one who decided she wanted to work in Deadwood. When she knocked on the door of a house there, she told the madam that Dell had said to look her up. The madam told her to go back and tell Dell Burke that she was too old to work."

"Isn't that the one who said, 'Oh yeah, give me one night to prove myself,' and the madam gave her the go-ahead?"

"That's the one." She turned back to the new girl. "By the time this old gal worked there twenty-four hours, she had knocked off more customers than that madam had ever seen, and she hired the girl on the spot. After that, the girl worked part-time in Deadwood and part-time in Lusk. Dell's a good trainer."

The new girl nodded. "I'm in the right place."

Local teenagers found various ways to approach the Yellow Hotel to satisfy their curiosity. Some came alone, some with friends. Some came aggressively and some more hesitantly. High school friends could get a guy in trouble or make memories like the time one boy was "run off" by Dell. On a dare, he knocked on the back door and walked inside down the hallway to the front waiting room where a girl stood. She asked if he wanted a drink, and he said, "No, I'm not old enough to drink."

Dell recognized him at once. "Young man, get out of my house. If you ever think about coming back, I'm gonna tell your dad."

Another teen had a different sort of experience with the hotel. Her uncle painted the 1949 Chevy he gave her robin's-egg blue before letting her have it, making it stand out when parked at the Dairy Bar where she worked. Her friends liked to snitch this car and park it close to Dell's back steps at the hotel. To retrieve her car, she sneaked through the bushes down the alley, crawled in her car, and started it while lying down in the seat. Then she roared out from the backyard, hoping no one noticed her coming from the Yellow Hotel in her "outstanding" vehicle.

Curiosity about the hotel came from all directions. The teenaged girl at the telephone office would call her friends to come listen in on calls to the brothel as they stifled their giggles. The male voices were numerous and easily identifiable.

At that time, telephone numbers were much simpler—it took only three digits to reach your party. Teenage boys thought it was a big deal to give Dell's number to the operator. After the phone rang but before anyone could answer, they would hang up. Other teenagers had another ploy. They sat up on the hill behind the hotel and watched as men entered Dell's establishment. When they recognized one, they raced down to the drugstore to phone the hotel and have the man paged. Occasionally, observers targeted the hotel for rock-throwing practice. Most boys were aware of the operations of the hotel by the age of eleven or twelve.

When two young boys knocked on the hotel door one day, Dell peered out through the curtained window. She was unsure who they were, but she opened the door a few inches and asked, "What do you want?"

The boys strained to see inside the darkened hotel. "We do odd jobs, and we wondered if you could use some help," one of the boys said. The other boy chimed in. "We could mow your lawn."

Dell's immediate answer was *"No!"* as she quickly shut the door.

Another time, some young men mischievously approached Dell "for a room." She answered politely, "We're full tonight. Perhaps you might find lodging at the Ranger."

A slumber party once included a call to the Yellow Hotel. The girls affected a southern accent and said they were new arrivals from Alabama looking for a job. Dell smiled as she heard laughter in the background. She carefully questioned the "girls" about their "experience in other brothels," but ended up telling them, "I'm sorry we don't have any current openings."

During one long and hard winter, Dell's girls became seriously ill with the flu. Dell's friend, Mrs. Fagan, who had met several of them at the hospital when they came in for physical exams, went to the Yellow Hotel and helped nurse them back to health. Dell paid her well; she knew her longtime friend needed the money.

A few days later, Mrs. Fagan and her friend Mrs. Barrett were walking down the street together and passed Dell Burke. Mrs. Fagan spoke to Dell. "Hello, how are you?"

"I'm fine, thank you. How are you?"

After the women had passed her, Mrs. Barrett asked in surprise, "Do you know her?"

Mrs. Fagan replied, "Yes, that's Dell Burke. We always speak."

Mrs. Barrett had not realized that a warm bond had developed between Dell and the Fagan family. Dell kept her close friendships private.

As the hard winter wore on, the cold drilled into the very bones of Luskites. "Time to head south," Dell told Jerry, suppressing a shiver. Snowdrifts were piling up and growing taller. The wind had picked up and the chill was becoming bitter. In April of 1952, they drove south through Arizona, making a short stop in Nogales.

From time to time, a beauty supply salesman from Cheyenne called at the Kut and Kurl beauty shop to show Evelyn Vollmer his new products. Occasionally, a salesman asked her husband, Bob, to help.

"This will make a difference in how you handle hair from now on," the salesman assured them as he showed them a new product. "It's for stripping the hair and tinting it blond."

"Aw heck, Evelyn. This looks easy, why don't ya become a blonde?" Bob suggested.

Bob and the salesman eventually talked her into it. They stripped Evelyn's hair, put a blue tint to it, and fixed her "all purty" with a permanent.

On Monday the beauty shop was full of customers, many of them older women who were clucking their tongues about the young girls stripping their hair like that. Dell was quietly sitting under a hair dryer when Bob came by to check the mail.

"Why'd you let her do that?" one older lady demanded of him.

Bob grinned. "Heck, I was the one that done it!" Gasps were heard around the room, and most of the women began to mutter. Bob spoke up. "But there's one thing I don't like about it!"

"What's that?" someone asked.

"If I wake up middle of the night and look over there and see that blonde I may think 'Oh, hell, I gotta get out of here and go home.'"

The women went silent. Covert glances slid toward Dell. Before he left, Dell called him over and said quietly, "Bob, you said the wrong thing!"

Bob had known Dell since childhood. Every year, she sent a Christmas card to Bob and Evelyn, containing a $10 bill in it. She always included a note saying, "Half of this is Bob's."

Thanksgiving 1952 was not a happy one. Jerry and Dell spent the days before the holiday and the actual holiday at the hospital with Jerry's mother, Melissa, where she lay dying. The day after Thanksgiving they finally sat down at the table at the country place. The turkey stuck in Jerry's throat and Dell passed up the gravy. They had so wanted it to be joyous for her, but his mother would never celebrate another one with them.

"It's kinda strange just being the two of us," Jerry said, looking down at his plate.

"Your mom was always here or we'd be over there for dinner."

"Now she's gone."

"Yeah, we're both orphans now. Funny idea, isn't it? My folks died so long ago, yet it doesn't seem that long since I got word . . . "

They sat silently for a while, and then Jerry spoke quietly. "At least, she's at peace." Dell nodded and reached for his hand.

By 1950 the Yellow Hotel had been in operation for more than thirty years, and it had gained considerable notice across the state and region. Almost all county residents were aware of its existence and where-abouts although they still held differing opinions on the operation itself. Some felt it was a distinction to have a house of ill repute within the county because there were few brothels still in operation. And the Yellow Hotel was, in its own way, becoming famous—or if not famous, at least infamous. It was almost a tourist attraction. Others ignored the hotel wishing it would just go away. And they avoided the madam who quietly went about her business.

Even so, there were still some residents who did not recognize Dell on the street, such as Dan Christian's mother, who one day stood chatting with a lady at the produce stand in the grocery store for some while. Afterwards, she walked up to a salesperson and asked, "Who's the lady over there? I've been visiting with her for about thirty minutes. She knows more about things that went on in this county than I do and I was born and raised here. She's such a nice lady."

The salesperson told her, "That's Dell Burke."

Mrs. Christian was shocked. "I would never have guessed. She is a real lady."

In 1952 the state of Wyoming enacted legislation requiring residents to obtain driver's licenses. Current drivers older than age sixteen were grandfathered in, meaning they were not required to take driving tests. It appears that when Dell applied for her driver's license, she listed her birth date as July 5, 1897, nine years after the actual date of 1888.

She delayed applying for a Social Security number until 1953 after she turned sixty-five. (Social Security had been available since 1940 for persons age sixty-five or older.) Dell was an attractive woman who still did not look her age; she probably did not want to admit she was in her sixties even then.

Dell could see at first glance that the man at the door was angry. "What're you doing here?" she asked him.

"My wife's totally unreasonable. She wants everything her way, wants to know everything I do, and never leaves me alone . . ." he began.

"Big fight, huh?"

"Worst one ever. She told me to get out and don't come back, so I figured I'd just come over here and show her a thing or two," he said belligerently.

"No," Dell said. "I don't want a family feud on my hands. Go on back home. You apologize to her and make peace."

He started to argue, "But, Dell, she's so . . . "

She wouldn't hear of it. "I won't be responsible for your divorce."

Dell's concerned side came out in other ways, too. She and Connie Panno had become friends, and they often shared a cup of coffee at Connie's flower shop in the Ranger Hotel. The two were so close that when Connie's daughter, Jean, graduated from high school in 1953, Dell gave her a place setting of her sterling silverware.

"Remember the first time we met?" Connie asked Dell one day over a cup of coffee.

Dell nodded. "You were so upset you almost cried as you left the hotel."

"I did cry as I walked down the street. I couldn't understand why you wouldn't let me stay there." They exchanged a wry glance and began laughing.

"I know. Town Marshall DeCastro told me about finding you on the street, looking like you were completely lost, and taking you over to the Silver Cliff. You hadn't been here long, had you?"

"No, I'd come from Italy a few months before and my folks had sent me some money I wanted to put in the bank, so my husband told me how to handle it. He said ride the train into town and go past the depot to the hotel, where I could get a room and stay overnight."

"He forgot about my hotel, didn't he?"

"He did. When I saw the word HOTEL on a tall yellow building I walked up to the front door and knocked."

"I remember seeing you there, scared, holding onto papers and a suitcase. Saying something about wanting a room."

"And then you said, 'No,' and more, but the only word I understood was no, and I thought you wouldn't let me in because I was an immigrant and didn't speak good English."

"I couldn't let you stay there. No one would have understood."

"Marshall DeCastro took me over to the other hotel and the lady there explained. I was so flustered I almost cried again."

Dell shook her head and smiled at her friend. "What a way to meet. And now you run this flower shop."

"Yes, I do. Have another cup of coffee?"

"Thanks."

It was Christmas up and down Main Street on a snowy day in the mid-1950s. The street was filled with holiday excitement. Dell wandered into shops, picking up a scarf, a sweater, or a small piece of jewelry, gifts for her girls. Coast-to-Coast Hardware featured gaily colored Christmas lights and decorations with music to set a seasonal mood. Shelves were filled not only with power tools, but also with toys, furniture, television sets and radios, and pots and pans, all designed to tantalize gift givers. While Dell browsed for gifts, she came across child-sized furniture. "Look at that little turquoise couch! It's so cute," she exclaimed. "There's even a place to put toys in it." She turned to the salesgirl. "I want one of these for my dog. Won't he be pleased on Christmas?"

The girl was surprised. "Could I help you find toys to put inside before we wrap it up?"

Dell was delighted. "Yes. Let's do that." Excitedly, they selected several items for her beloved dog. Dell pulled out her purse and counted out the money in $5 bills. The salesgirl smiled as she helped carry the gifts to Dell's car.

The next stop was the grocery store. Dell had learned that many people could not afford a good meal for Christmas and she made it an annual event to stop at the Safeway grocery store to carefully select what she believed would provide one. Then she called Sheriff Jugler, told him the baskets would be ready the next day, and asked him to pick them up for her. He brought them by the country place the following day and received the list telling where he was to deliver them. Anonymously, they were handed over or left on doorsteps.

Dell was prudent how she spent her money. At the same time, she was a generous tipper and made sure her girls were, too. At the beauty shops, they were considered very good customers. When Lonnie Allen worked at the Texaco just down from the hotel, he was called on to service Dell's car. After the work was complete, he returned the car to the hotel. Dell always thanked him and pressed a silver dollar into his hand.

Winters in Wyoming were very cold, and snow piled up in deep banks along the roads and around houses. Hotel business generally slowed down, making it an ideal time to vacation. Jerry and Dell often traveled to California during this time. Two ladies from Sundance, 115 miles north of Lusk, also enjoyed winter trips to California. They usually stayed in what was reputed to be the best hotel in town. Each day after they dressed up they went down and sat in the lobby, where one day they noticed an attractive small lady.

"Where are you from?" one of the ladies from Sundance asked the woman.

She said, "Lusk, Wyoming."

Excited to find a fellow Wyomingite, the lady asked, "Do you know the Percivals? They're from Lusk."

"Well, I've heard of them," the woman admitted. "Actually, the only one I know is Roger . . . he has a liquor store there."

The ladies kept talking to Dell. They couldn't figure out why she was so pleasant to them while not allowing them to make any headway with her. They noticed that sometimes she met a man and left with him.

After they returned to Wyoming, the ladies asked the Percivals about this Luskite. Betty Percival recognized their description of the lady in the lobby. "That was Dell Burke from the Yellow Hotel."

On May 12, 1955, Dell wrote a $300 check to the Highway Garage for a deposit on a New Yorker Chrysler Sedan. On June 14 she wrote a check for $2,500, which was marked "Paid in Full for Chrysler 1955 New Yorker DeLuxe, to the Highway Garage." Other records indicate that she considered selling the 1940 Packard for $400.

About a month later, the front page of *The Lusk Herald* carried the story of a life-changing event for Dell. The headline proclaimed: "Heart Attack Claims Jerry Dull at Wheel of Car Saturday Night: Last Services, Burial Conducted Tuesday."

It had begun like any other Saturday night. Dell had gone to the hotel in the afternoon, and Jerry had gone to the Oasis to make sure everything was in place for the evening's activities. It was business as usual for both. A firm knock on the back door summoned Dell. The drawn face of Highway Patrolman Butch Jordan warned her something was wrong, and she quickly ushered him into the small waiting room.

"He died almost instantly," Butch told her. "I was right there, but I couldn't do a thing. It was over before I could get to him." Dell listened in shock as Butch talked. Jerry had been driving up Main Street to run back out to the country place, and his car had gone out of control. Apparently, he had a heart attack and crashed into a couple of parked cars in front of Pop's Diner. Butch had been parked in front of the Lusk Service Station and had seen Jerry collapse.

"But, he was perfectly healthy! I can't believe he had a heart attack," Dell protested.

Butch leaned over to her. "Come with me, Dell. I think you'll want to see him." The two of them hurried to the mortuary.

The sight of Jerry on the table was almost too much to bear. *Any minute now,* she thought, *he'll sit up, stretch, and say, 'Let's go home.'* But he didn't. He just lay there. Jerry was gone. She could see that the car accident hadn't really hurt him much.

"He was gone before his car hit, Dell," the patrolman said. "His heart gave out, and he let go."

So many arrangements to make, people to contact. Dell was too busy to feel. The funeral attracted people from all over. Numbly, Dell received their condolences and sympathy, and she talked with towns-people she usually avoided. Out-of-town visitors included Maude Jackson, Jerry's one surviving sister. She and her son had flown in from California for the funeral.

The next week, stories abounded at the wake that was held in the Oasis Bar. Dell's girls sat in the booths, visiting with all comers. Drinks and food flowed freely. She knew Jerry would have enjoyed that night with friends gathered around telling stories about him, about the times he had befriended or helped them, and about his practical jokes. After it was all over, there was time to think . . . and to feel. She read through the newspaper story again. It did not mention her name—his faithful companion and lover. She had known it wouldn't, but still it irked. She was a mourner without the right to grieve like his friends and his family—his closest friend could not openly grieve.

The girls knew she hurt deeply. At first they kept a distance, but gradually they came closer, and this afternoon two sat down with her, poured glasses of wine, and lifted them in silent acknowledgment.

Dell finally spoke. "God, I miss that man. I miss Jerry. I wish he was alive. Never mind all those times he . . . I would take him back in a minute if only . . . " Tears filled her eyes. Her head ached as she cried. She drew the wine into her mouth and rolled it over her tongue. "Wishing won't bring him back." She gulped tears back. "But, I can't help it. I miss him so much," she wailed. Her Pekingese looked solemnly up at her and snuggled close beside her on the couch. "We were gonna get married someday. But it's over and I just have to get used to it and go on." She closed her eyes and felt the tears flow down her face.

The girls moved closer to her and held her as she cried.

Jerry died intestate. He had never taken the time to put a will together, and this came back to haunt them all. Witnesses verified that Jerry had wanted Dell to have part of his estate should he die, and as a result she received one-third, with one-third going to his sister and the remaining one-third divided between two nephews.

In September, Dell sought legal advice from Tom Fagan, the son of her old friends, to represent Jerry's nephews. The estate was valued at $27,000 to $39,000, and it included numerous stocks Jerry had invested in. For the next several years, she worked closely with Attorney Judson P. Watson and his wife, Minerva, to settle related matters. One issue was the partnership Jerry had with Maynard Bishop's widow in the Oasis Bar and Club Billiards. Eventually, Dell sold her interest in these ventures to Bessie M. Bishop for $11,250. Now in her mid-sixties, Dell found managing the hotel, her country place, and other investments was all she could handle, and she was pleased to hand this off to Bessie.

With heavy heart, Dell silently signaled the change in her life when she wrote to her young great-niece Loraine, asking her to ". . . please address my mail to Dell Burke. I know this represents a bit of a change for you, but this is the name I go by. But to you, I'll always be your Aunt Marie, just as you will always be my little Loraine." Exactly why she requested this address change is still a mystery to her family, and Dell continued to have the Fisher family call her Marie when they spoke to her in person. She never discussed the two names with Loraine, although she made a point of keeping in touch with her great-niece.

Roy Fisher (Loraine's father) always stopped in Lusk to visit his Aunt Marie as his family went west on vacation. On arriving in Lusk, they usually met her at the hotel to pick up the key for the country place. Before leaving the hotel, Loraine looked at the painting in her great-aunt's large room. "That's an interesting picture of Devil's Tower. Is that new?" she asked.

"Not really. An Indian called Broken Rope painted it about six years ago. He used a house paintbrush to do most of his pictures. Over here I have another one he did of Big Thompson Canyon in Colorado."

"Do you have any more by him?"

"No, but he did a couple of murals for the Silver Cliff Hotel around 1950. Huge landscapes. Tall imposing mountains. Wide rivers flowing by. They're beautiful."

She turned to her nephew. "When you get out to the house, Roy, would you mind watering the flowers and trees for me?" It was another dry year.

"Sure, it'll be like old times." The family left the hotel bound for a weekend at the country place. Usually they ate dinner at the country place, but this time they went back into town and picked Marie up to go to a restaurant for dinner. Marie rarely introduced them to local people; just as the family knew little about her business life, few local people ever met her family.

Marie was adept at changing the subject if family asked questions whose answers might reveal too much. A question about hotel business might be answered with a general statement about how convenient the location was at a busy highway intersection, and then she might ask if they had ever seen an antelope herd so large they could not be counted, or a similar comment. The smooth transition away from personal information was rarely noticed. Thus she continued to maintain the separateness of her two lives, protect her professional identity, and spare her family embarrassment.

The grief, loss, and loneliness Dell felt with the passing of so many important people in her life was compounded by the death of her brother Herb in Seattle in 1958. Death had indeed become an enemy.

The crossroads location of the hotel was ideal and paid off not only for the hotel, but also for other businesses in Lusk. Not only did State Highways 85 and 20 intersect in Lusk with Highway 85 running within one block of the hotel, but in addition the hotel was across the street from the railway station.

Salesmen who had a choice of stopping in Torrington, Douglas, Newcastle, or Lusk often chose Lusk because they preferred the girls at Dell's hotel. This stop meant they would rent a motel room and have dinner somewhere in town, often accompanied by shopping for other sundries.

In 1955 the natural gas pipeliners who came through the area were a rugged crew. As the pipeline progressed, they moved away from Lusk and closer to Newcastle. But even after the construction bosses moved their headquarters north to Newcastle, many of the men kept coming back to Lusk.

"Those pipeliners get pretty rough . . . " Dell told Kester Akers, who had made several electrical repairs for Dell recently.

"What did they tear up this time?" Kester asked.

"The big kid didn't like having such a short time with Lotty, and he ripped the wires right off the timer clock."

Kester was sitting on the stairs working over the wiring when Lotty strolled downstairs later. Wearing a skimpy nightie, she yawned and asked him, "Whatcha doin'?"

"Guess your sweetie got a little rough last night." He grinned.

Dell stepped in and scolded Lotty. "What are you doing down here like that, young lady? Get dressed." Lotty shot a dark look at her boss and scooted back upstairs.

Kester smiled, remembering the days when he delivered newspapers to the hotel. Dell had often had cookies and hot chocolate waiting for him when he came to collect the paper money.

The year after Jerry died, Doc Reckling told Dell about Red Fenwick, the *Denver Post* columnist who had written a new book called *Red Fenwick's West*. "He's coming to Lusk for an autograph party. You should meet him."

"You could bring him down here," Dell suggested.

Doc showed up with Red Fenwick in tow, and Red inscribed one of his books for her: "To a lovely little lady in red velvet who perhaps more eloquently than any other woman, can testify to the masculinity of a truly masculine state, Wyoming."

"That's so sweet. How about sending me more of those books?" Dell asked. "When these cowboys come in to see my girls, I'll sell 'em a book."

Fenwick did, and later she ordered additional copies. He visited her each time he came through town. "Doc Reckling thinks I should write a book about you," he told Dell on one of his visits.

"I don't think so," she demurred. "I know too much about too many prominent people in Wyoming, including politicians, public officials, businessmen, and the like." It was often suspected that Dell did know important people throughout the region and the state, as well as nationwide. And that some of them were her customers.

During the time Harve Ledford managed the Foster Lumber Company from 1950 to 1965, Dell frequently stopped by for supplies and for construction help. Summer hailstorms damaged glass windows at both houses, and other repairs were sometimes needed. One such time was a hot Saturday night when the cowboys became especially unruly. Dell kept an eye on one loud, tall, dark-haired boy. When he finished his third whiskey, she ushered him to the back door. He must have gone around to the front of the hotel, because the next thing she heard was a commotion on the front porch.

"You can't stop me from seeing her!"

"Yes, I can!" came the reply, followed by loud thumps and a crash. Dell peered through the window in the front door as she signaled one of the girls to call the sheriff. By the time the sheriff arrived, the dark-haired boy was gone but a blonde one lay groaning on the lawn beside the porch railing he must have crashed through.

The next morning Dell visited Foster Lumber Company. The

porch needed repairs. "As a matter of fact," she told Harve, "I'd like someone to come out and do it today, if possible."

Harve called his regular carpenter over to the store. When the job was described, the carpenter reacted strongly. "No, I can't do that."

"Why not?" Harve asked.

"My wife would kill me," the carpenter responded.

Harve kept talking because he knew the man needed the work. Finally they came to an agreement. That afternoon he said, "Harve, I told my wife I'll be working here at the lumberyard all afternoon, so if she calls, tell her I'm busy, but you'll have me call her back. And you call me at the hotel." The man didn't want to lose out on the work and income, but he knew his wife would be very upset if she was aware he was working at the Yellow Hotel.

Katherine Wood kept the lumberyard accounts, sent out bills, cut glass, and took lumber orders at the Foster Lumber Company for some years. But she did not cut lumber.

One afternoon, Dell came in and ordered eight pieces of plywood.

"Cut two feet off the ends, which makes four by eights into four by sixes. I want to use them for the beds because the girls like them firm."

Katherine wrote down the order. When her co-worker came back from lunch, she gave him the order and asked him to cut and deliver the plywood.

"You're putting me on," the man said. "If this isn't right, you'll have to pay for it."

"This is no joke. That's what she wants."

After he cut the plywood and put it in his truck, the man glanced at the clock and noted the time.

Katherine grinned. "You could leave them at the back door, if you want to. But it would be nice to help the girls put them under the mattresses. Those are heavy awkward pieces for them to lift."

He was not gone long. When he returned, Katherine asked him, "Did you put the plywood under the mattresses?"

"No, by God, they can do that themselves." He was so adamant, Katherine had to chuckle. She had met Dell only as a customer at the lumberyard and enjoyed visiting with her there. Dell always paid cash, and the store never had to send out a bill. One day Katherine spoke to Dell on the street.

Dell told her, "When you meet me on the street, you don't speak to me."

"I don't really understand that. I want to greet you wherever I meet you." Katherine wanted to be friends, but as usual Dell kept her distance.

Virginia Watson, a manicurist who tended Dell's nails at the beauty shop, ran into Dell at the post office one day. Dell was carrying a load of packages, and Virginia stopped to help her. After the packages were deposited in the car, Dell turned to her and said, "Sweetie, you don't do this."

Virginia was puzzled. "Do what?"

"When we're downtown, you don't speak to me."

"Why not?"

"You know my trade. You know my profession."

Virginia answered, "If I'm good enough to do your hair and you're nice enough to come up to the shop, then I will speak to you downtown when I see you."

To Virginia's surprise, Dell said, "I would really rather you didn't."

However, this injunction was sharply different from a later meeting when Virginia was working at a salon in Denver. Virginia was walking through the salon when an arm came out from under the dryer and grabbed her. It was Dell, in Denver buying supplies, where she felt free to have a long personal conversation with the manicurist.

In the 1950s, numerous high school seniors registered for the draft and received draft notices upon finishing high school. Two eighteen-year-old friends who had received their notices were still too young to get in the bars legally, but they decided to go to Dell's Hotel, anyway. At the door, Dell informed them, "You're too young to come in here."

"But we just got our draft notices, and we're going into the service to defend our country . . . "

She hesitated a moment. "Then I guess you're old enough to come in."

They went into the parlor to wait. When one boy's turn came, Dell took him up the steps. About that time somebody was coming down. The boy was embarrassed and covered his face. But when they got side by side, the boy took a peek to see who was beside him. He looked over and met his father's eyes. He never mentioned it to his father, and the father never mentioned it to the boy.

Dell tried to prevent such embarrassing moments, but sometimes it seemed almost unavoidable. Living a dual life herself, she probably could understand a similar desire her customers had for their anonymity. It was a delicate dance keeping the local males, numerous businessmen, the youth, and others in the community all satisfied. The loss of Jerry Dull probably made her situation even more uncomfortable as this confidant had undoubtedly been of great support.

Fisher Family in Ohio (circa 1885). From left to right: Mary Ada (Marie/Dell), Almeda (Mother), John (Father), Herb, Charlie, and Burl.

*Marie and
Stephen J. Law,
circa 1905.*

A young Dell Burke/Marie Fisher.

The Fisher family on one of Marie's trips to visit her siblings.

Dell (circa 1920)
fashionably dressed in
the latest styles.

Dell (circa 1920)
always dressed elegantly.

Dell and her friend Jerry Dull relaxing on vacation in Mexico.

*Dell loved her Pekingese dogs
as if they were children.*

*Among other quiet good deeds, Dell was rumored to have underwritten the Lusk
Power Plant in 1929.*

Fine amber-colored rhinestones Dell may have worn, a recent photograph of the Yellow Hotel, and brothel tokens.

Dell in the 1940s, wearing her ermine-trimmed fur muff.

The doorbell from the Yellow Hotel, with a period coin purse and brothel tokens.

BUSINESS AS USUAL, 1960–1969

Sundays stretched out endlessly with the hotel closed on that day. One Sunday in the early 1960s, Dell walked across town to the motel run by Hester Smith and her son, Bill. She wanted to ask Bill about doing work at the country place, and it was a good excuse for a visit. Soon Dell was seated on the porch with a cup of coffee in hand.

While Dell always included Hester in their conversations, Bill was the one who talked more with her. Hester picked up the handiwork she always kept nearby.

After Dell and Bill arranged a time for Bill to do the necessary work, they began discussing politics. Dell held strong opinions about the hypocrisy she found in the political system and favored the Republicans. She was often critical of the governors, even though Governor Stan Hathaway was reportedly one of Dell's personal attorneys who took care of her legal matters in the 1960s.

The rest of the conversation ranged from weather to the new minister in town who wanted to close her down. "This usually happens when a church brings in a new preacher." Dell was philosophical, but regretful. "You know, Bill," she said, "people look down on me because of my business, but if it wasn't for me, there wouldn't be any lights now."

"I know, Dell. He'll back off pretty soon. They always do."

Population was down in Lusk but new businesses were still coming in. Most of them made a go of it. Oil production stabilized at a high plateau in the 1960s and was forecast to continue into the next decade.

In 1960 Don Whiteaker became manager of his family's business, the Whiteaker Clothing Store in Lusk. Initiation for new businessmen was to solicit funds for the Lusk Chamber of Commerce. Not only did that raise money for the chamber, but it also introduced newcomers to the other business owners.

Don glanced over his list and saw Dell's name. "Here I am," he thought, "trying to be a respected businessperson on Main Street, and I have the Yellow Hotel." He was dismayed. Most businesses on Main Street paid $25 to $50 a year for membership in the chamber of commerce. Since it was his first visit, he asked other members how much Dell should pay. He was told $200.

The next day he called on Dell. "I'm here for the Lusk Chamber of Commerce."

"How much do they want this year?" Dell inquired.

"Well, they suggested $200 . . . " Don stopped and held his breath. Dell laughed and paid that amount—in $5 bills.

That was the beginning of their friendship. Dell enjoyed his company and conversation and often shared tales of her adventures with him. The two found morning was a good time to trade local gossip. When they talked, Don often was struck by the "nowness" of what she discussed. She rarely mentioned her past or her business. And although they talked freely at the hotel, Dell never acknowledged him on the street.

When the phone rang early in the week, Don recognized Dell's voice as she inquired, "What would be a good day for the girls to shop?"

"It's quiet right now," Don answered, "and it doesn't look like this'll be a busy day. Want to come on over?"

Dell and two of her girls soon arrived.

"We have a new shipment of blouses." Don pointed toward a table at the side of the store. "If you need help, let me know."

The salesgirl standing near the table abruptly turned and walked away. She would have refused to wait on Dell or her girls if asked. Don knew this and took the orders himself.

Dell always brought her dog, Yen Chee, wearing a brightly colored ribbon around his neck, shopping with her. The dog always smelled of perfume, as did Dell and the girls.

Not long after Merle and Phyllis Hahn began managing the Gamble's Hardware Store in 1960, a young girl wearing a formfitting orange pantsuit came in with a small dog draped over her arm. Phyllis walked over and asked, "May I help you?" She noted that although the girl had a very attractive body, her face did not match. The girl emanated a pleasant, expensive perfume, but locally raised Phyllis could not place her face.

The girl selected a radio marked $20. "I have $10 with me. Could I pay the rest in two weeks?"

As usual Phyllis turned to Merle to approve the credit request, and he began his routine credit check. "Well, I don't know you. Where do you work and what do you do?"

The girl paused and stuttered, "W-w-well, I work for Dell Burke."

Merle said, "I don't know Dell Burke. What do you do?" He glanced over at his wife, who recognized Dell's name and was turning all shades of red.

The girl stammered as she repeated, "I-I-I work for Dell Burke."

Suddenly, Merle realized what was going on and quickly approved the girl's credit.

As a newcomer to Lusk in 1961, Al Tichener considered it good business to join local organizations, and he chose the Lions Club, Boy Scouts, and Fire Department. Each one appealed to the community regularly for support, and Al was asked to visit Dell for all of them. Within one month, he appeared at her back door three times. The first time, he spoke for the Boy Scouts. She invited him inside the hall and went into the kitchen for a contribution. The second time, he represented the Lions Club. The same procedure occurred. As he approached the hotel for a third time, he felt a bit daunted by the repetition and told Dell, "I'm here asking for money again. It seems like all I do is knock on your door and ask for money."

"Well, you certainly don't spend any here," Dell teased.

He gulped and nodded. "This time, it's for the Fire Department."

"Why didn't you say so?" She led him down the hall to her parlor and prepared a glass of whiskey. They talked about their travels and her shopping trips to Denver. She described what Lusk was like when she first arrived. She told about the men who knocked at her back door during the Depression. "You know, I never turned one down. People said I was foolish giving away food, but when times got better, it paid tenfold."

Dell appreciated the Fire Department and compensated them well.

On a pleasant Saturday afternoon, Diane, one of Dell's girls, left the hotel and strolled down the street. Stepping into a bar, her peasant blouse and full skirt showed off her body both discreetly and fully. She sat down beside one of the regulars who was there slurping down a beer. After a while, she moved to another table and then another. Finally, she worked her way around the entire room and reached the counter. "You know, everyone in here is a friend of mine. See that they all have a drink on me," she told the bartender. He grinned, and she winked at him. She settled onto a bar stool for a chat while she sipped a soda.

When she finished her drink, she turned and surveyed the room before reaching into the top of her bra where barely out of sight was a roll of $5 bills. "How much for one more round for my friends?" she asked the bartender. He named a price, and she counted out the richly perfumed bills before handing them to him. All eyes were on her as she picked her way toward the door. Pausing a moment there, she turned and said softly with a slightly affected Southern accent, "Y'all come over and see me tonight."

A middle-aged man in a business suit stepped up to the bar. "Whoa! Who was that?"

"That's Diane. She works at Dell's Hotel."

"Where's that? I was headed there when I stopped in."

As the man walked out the door, the bartender turned to a regular sitting on a barstool. "See! Happened again." He swiped at the counter with a rag. "I send so many guys over to that hotel, I feel like an unpaid pimp." Throughout Lusk, restaurateurs, salespeople, motel owners, filling-station attendants, and others provided directions to the Yellow Hotel.

Various men arriving in Lusk for business or pleasure needed a place to stay. One evening Opal was clearing the table at the Silver Dollar Bar when the man seated at the table asked, "When I got off the train, I seen a hotel across the street. Any rooms for rent down there?"

Unsure whether the question was serious, Opal picked up the empty bottles. "Why don't you go down and see? I couldn't tell you myself."

For the ten years Opal and Eddie Plumb operated the Silver Dollar Bar, they dealt with this question from time to time. Opal was always embarrassed by it, and at times she suggested one of the other hotels and motels.

And then there were the girls, pretty ladies who slipped in for an afternoon drink.

"Can't drink a real one at the hotel," the brunette with long curls remarked. Her companion nodded. The brunette turned to Opal as drinks were placed on the table. "You won't tell Dell we're here, will you?"

"No, I won't tell Dell."

The girls usually had one or two drinks and went back to the hotel before they could be missed.

One local businessman thought it was fun to give Dell Burke's phone number to traveling salesmen who needed a room for the night. When they called, Dell explained what her business was, and generally the salesman found lodging elsewhere. At times, she went so far as to call other hotels or motels to see if room was available. When Dell called the Smiths, the response depended on who answered. Hester tended to say, "I'm sorry, but we're full tonight." Her husband, Bill, always said, "Sure, send them up."

The young men of Lusk were naturally curious about the activities that went on at the Yellow Hotel, and one night a boy decided it was time to visit Dell Burke.

"You can't do that!" some of his friends disagreed.

"Oh yeah," he replied. "Watch me."

The bantering continued until the boys were at the door of the Yellow Hotel, where Dell met them and took them into the parlor. She offered them a soda, and asked about their brothers, their fathers, their uncles. She seemed to know the men in their families by name.

Later that evening, the boys shared other experiences. One older boy told about a night he had gone to the hotel. Dell led him to a seat, handed him a drink, and said, "You'll have to wait awhile. All the girls are busy, but someone will be free soon." When two girls came into the room with two men, he looked closely to see if he knew any of them. Suddenly, he slunk down into the chair, head on his chest. One man was his father.

Boys who knocked on the hotel door heard differing responses. "Go home and don't come back," Dell told one. Others were told, "Come back when you grow up, but for now, get the hell out of here. You're too young."

As Chris (not his real name) listened to the guys, he knew what he could do to get bragging rights. The other guys would look up to him for going to the hotel. Not just for going there, some had already done that. Yes, he would be the first to go upstairs. The next day he pressed the hotel's doorbell. A petite auburn-haired lady he was sure must be Dell opened the door and inspected him quickly. "Are you of age to drink?" she demanded. He gulped as he answered, "Yes'm, I am." She led him down the narrow hall to a large room where music came from the jukebox. He glanced around at the benches, chairs, and sofas lining the room.

"How's your family, Chris?" Dell seemed to know him even before he spoke, and they discussed ranching, calving, and the latest

movies. Then Dell asked, "Would you like to meet the girls?" He nod-
ded and looked down. Soon, three young women came into the room.
He grinned at the curly haired blonde in a short blue dress. "That's
Sandy. She's a sweet girl," Dell told him.

Although Sandy promised to teach him how to dance, Chris was
too nervous to even try and was beginning to wonder if he'd made a
mistake. Sandy leaned over and whispered, "Dell said this was your first
time, and we can go real slow if you want to." Chris felt his face get
hot. "Want to go upstairs?" she softly invited. He nodded.

The lights were dim in the sparsely furnished bedroom. Beside
the washstand that held a pitcher of fresh water stood an iron twin bed
covered with a clean white sheet. It began like in the movies.
Afterward, they lay quietly, both panting. Chris looked over at Sandy
in awe, "Wow."

She smiled and rolled over as a bell rang nearby and downstairs
at the callbox. "Come back and see me," she invited.

Bragging rights? Yeah. Now he had real bragging rights about
the Yellow Hotel. And probably he wasn't the only one for whom this
story played out for the young men in Lusk in the mid-1960s.

As Dell spread her fingers out for a manicure at Kut and Kurl, she
glanced up at the lady who walked in. This was probably the wife of
the new minister, who had recently moved to Lusk. Seeing Dell sitting
there, the lady asked, "What's your name?"

"I'm Dell Burke."

The newcomer said, "My husband's a new preacher here. What
do you do?" Beauty operator Dorothy Jordan became nervous, know-

ing where this could lead. She tried to move the lady past Dell to avoid embarrassment, but the newcomer stood waiting for Dell to speak.

"I have a hotel."

"Oh, what hotel is this?"

Eventually, Dell said, "The Yellow Hotel."

"Where's that?" the woman asked, and Dell motioned over the hill as Dorothy finally managed to lead the lady toward the back of the salon.

The wives of all the ministers in Lusk held regular ecumenical meetings. At one meeting, the new pastor's wife sat quietly until the leader asked if anyone had anything else to say.

The newcomer spoke up. "This town has an evil influence living here. Dell Burke brings shame to Lusk and the Yellow Hotel should be closed down." She continued her diatribe against prostitution, Dell Burke, and the hotel. She called on the other wives to help.

When she sat down, she waited, but no one spoke. The subject never came up again. Although it went unsaid, rumor had it that most or all of the churches benefited in some way from Dell's generosity, from new windows to support for various building projects.

For the next few years, Dell operated as usual. She continued to make improvements to the hotel, attend to personal matters, and contribute to the community. During a visit to a Denver hotel, Dell noticed a bench that she could use to seat waiting customers. On December 12, 1961, she received an invoice from Northwestern Railway Company for a leather settee. Several of these leather benches became prized possessions during her estate sale in 1981.

In 1962 when she applied for Social Security benefits, Dell's subterfuge about her age haunted her. At age seventy-five she applied to receive Social Security, apparently revealing her real birth date, and she was able to receive a year's retroactive payment.

In November 1962, Dell wrote a check for $1,219.70 to the Spencer Hospital for a forty-three-day stay, during which Doc Reckling had tended her dislocated shoulder and double fracture of the wrist. Nothing more is known about this incident.

Dell continued to support the community. In 1962 she gave $15 to the Babe Ruth Baseball team for uniforms and $50 to St. Paul's Lutheran Church for their Building Fund. The following year, she sent $470 to her distant cousin, Charles Hartwig, for tuition to Stanford University.

Dell also contributed money to help erect a monument to Mother Featherlegs, who had operated a "way station" on the stagecoach line between the Black Hills of South Dakota and Cheyenne, Wyoming. In 1879 Mother Featherlegs was murdered for a stash she was holding, and later Russell Thorpe, a former stage driver, validated her grave between that of desperadoes George McFadden and Ike Diapert. A rock pile on the Ord ranch south of Lusk marks the final resting place of this notorious woman. Bob Darrow managed the Ord ranch, and his family occasionally invited Jim Griffith, the editor of *The Lusk Herald*, and his family for dinner at the ranch. On an evening early in 1964, Mary Ann Griffith grew weary of hearing the men complain that Mother Featherlegs's resting place had not received appropriate notice. "Either do something or quit talking about it," she threatened the men. They decided to erect a monument.

A stone was donated by Lake Harris, who operated a stone monument business in nearby Jay Em, and he requested $100 to sandblast the epitaph on it. Jeannette Sager and Gertrude Chamberlain each contributed $25, but Jim and Bob needed to find someone to donate the rest of the money. Jim called Dell, who agreed to provide the remaining $50.

Lew Bates, editor of the *Wyoming State Tribune* in Cheyenne, noted "the uniqueness of the monument and even the dedication ceremony." Women from the Jay Em community church served lunch at the event. The original "guesstimate" of a couple hundred attendees was not equal to the 750 who showed up, and make-do meals had to be prepared. Before Russell Thorpe unveiled the monument by pulling a rawhide thong from a pair of red pantalettes, he paused. With his hand on the edge of the pantalettes-covered stone, Thorpe commented, "You know, I wasn't asked what to put on this monument. But, if I had been, this is what I'd have said:

> HERE LIES CHARLOTTE.
>
> BORN A VIRGIN, SHE DIED A HARLOT.
>
> FOR THIRTEEN LONG YEARS
>
> SHE KEPT HER VIRGINITY.
>
> AND THAT'S ONE HELLUVA RECORD
>
> FOR THIS VICINITY.

With that he pulled the thong to reveal the epitaph, which read:

> HERE LIES
>
> MOTHER FEATHERLEGS
>
> SHEPHERD
>
> SO CALLED AS IN HER
>
> RUFFLED PANTALETTES
>
> SHE LOOKED LIKE A

FEATHER-LEGGED

CHICKEN IN A HIGH WIND

WAS A ROADHOUSE MA'AM

HERE ON THE CHEYENNE

BLACK HILLS STAGE LINE

AN OUTLAW CONFEDERATE

SHE WAS MURDERED BY

DANGEROUS DICK DAVIS

THE TERRAPIN IN 1879

FOR A $1500 CACHE

DEDICATED MAY 17, 1964

Although Dell chose not to attend the dedication, she wanted to see the monument. A year later, one of her girls and her Pekingese joined her for the drive south in her Chrysler New Yorker. The sky was heavy with chilly moisture. Bob Darrow and Jim Griffith met them at the highway and led the way in a truck. But as they left the main road, Dell's car became mired in the mud, so the women and dog joined the men in the truck. A hard rain soon sent them back to the Ord ranch to warm up.

Later, Bob let Yen Chee, Dell's beloved Pekingese, out to relieve himself, but Yen did not come back. This worried Dell. She had trained Yen Chee to come to a referee's whistle, but he did not respond.

The rain subsided about sunset, and Jim took the women back to town, leaving dog and car behind. Dell was deeply upset. The next morning, the Darrows were wakened by neighbors walking along the creek whistling for the dog.

Dell phoned nearby radio stations and placed notices in the Lusk and Torrington newspapers. She called Bill Barker, the morning personality on KOA radio in Denver. She posted a sign on the hotel saying it was closed until the dog was found.

She bought all the referee whistles she could find in town, and spread the word for local sheepherders and cowboys to come help. In the meantime the Darrows left for the Wyoming Stockgrowers Convention in Laramie.

Troops of men teetered up and down over the pine-topped hills in high-heeled cowboy boots, blowing on whistles for several days. Because it was coyote and bobcat country, everyone believed the dog was gone. After the Darrows returned from the convention, they turned their basset hounds out. They found the Pekingese less than a hundred yards from the house, bedraggled but alive. Bob carried it into the house and with great relief called Dell. Almost immediately she was at his door with arms open wide to greet her beloved pet. She looked the animal over closely. "He's cold but he looks okay. I'm so glad you found him."

Doc Reckling died of a heart condition in 1964, and Dell was forced to find a new physician. Sometimes she took her girls to Dr. Torkelson. For other medical problems, she chose other doctors. The nurses and aides were amused by payments made in $5 bills. One new doctor commented, "Everybody told me that Dell was only the madam . . . that she didn't take customers. But she came in and got her health examination, too. I think the original merchandise is still in use." Or, at the least, she chose to be a good role model. Many people wondered whether Dell continued actively in her profession; however, this was never actually validated.

Dell generally shopped in Lusk for what she needed. This

included blinds, rugs, and appliances at Gamble's Hardware Store, clothing at Whiteakers, groceries at Safeway, and other items throughout town. Sometimes her girls shopped downtown, too.

She bought two refrigerators from Gamble's during their thirty-five years of business. She usually paid in cash. When she bought the first one, Merle Hahn put the bills in the cash drawer and later noticed the salesgirl picking her way carefully through the drawer to avoid making change with any of the highly perfumed bills.

When Dell traded the refrigerator in on a new one, another saleslady was asked to clean up the old one. She scrubbed the appliance for two days before she considered it ready for resale. About a year after Dell bought the second appliance, she stopped by the store and told Merle, "You know, I should have bought one with an ice maker. Could you install one in the fridge I got from you?" As usual, Dell glanced at Merle's wife to make sure it would be acceptable for Merle to work at the hotel. Phyllis smiled and nodded.

One of Dell's girls came into the kitchen to watch while Merle installed the icemaker in the hotel refrigerator. "How's business?" she asked him. When Merle replied that business was good, the girl commented, "Mine isn't too good." Then she added, "I think the girls up at Casper are undercutting my prices." The conversation left the hardware-store owner speechless.

Archie Lauer worked for Cy Bonner at his paint shop in the mid-1960s. House-painting business was slow, so Archie looked about for jobs. As he drove past the Yellow Hotel on his way to Bonner's shop, he noticed the hotel could use a coat of paint. He knew that Dell liked to keep the yellow color bright, so he suggested to Cy that they approach Dell and ask if they could paint the hotel. Cy agreed, and

Archie returned to the Yellow Hotel. Dell opened the front door when he knocked, and her response to his inquiry was, "Sure, why not?" The men appreciated the business and were grateful when it was done. As usual Dell paid promptly. Archie was not really sure whether the hotel had needed the paint job or Dell knew Bonner's Paint Shop needed the business, but he was grateful for the work.

Shortly after an aspiring young lawyer came to Lusk to open his practice, he accepted the job as city attorney He noticed that a brothel was operating in full swing in Lusk and visited with the police chief about the illegal business. "I'd like you to go arrest Madam Burke," he informed the chief.

The amiable chief said, "Sure, I'll go do that," and left the office.

Within a few minutes, the lawyer's phone rang. It was the mayor. Following casual chitchat, the mayor asked, "How ya liking your job?"

"I'm really liking it. It's a good job and I'm enjoying it."

The mayor proceeded. "Ya want to keep your job?"

This sounded ominous. The new city attorney said slowly, "Yeah, I want to keep my job."

The mayor spoke firmly. "Then leave Dell Burke alone. She's never hurt anybody in this town, and we don't have rape and other such things here because of her running that place." Like others before him and after him, the attorney never pursued it further.

Because of her earlier experience with Dell, Flora Huff was not put off when she found one of Dell's girls in the hospital. The girl lay quietly in the small sterile bed at Dr. Torkelson's hospital. Flora had been working at the hospital as a nurse since the death of her husband a couple years earlier and was curious as to what was the matter with the young lady.

"What's wrong with her?" she asked.

"That's one of Dell's girls, and she has the flu," the head nurse responded, and then she turned to the other nurses standing around her. "Here're the straws. Let's see who has to work with her." Flora held her breath and drew the short one. Remembering Dell as a neighbor and benefactress, she was excited.

When Flora came out of the girl's room, she exclaimed, "You know, she's very nice." The rest of the girl's stay was an easy task for Flora. In time the girl recovered and went back to work. Shortly after that a huge box of chocolates arrived at the hospital, marked FOR THE NURSES.

A few days later, Flora ran into the girl at the drugstore. She was surprised that the girl turned her head and did not speak. Flora decided that the hotel privacy rule must be much like confidentiality was at the hospital. After she had come to know several of Dell's girls, whom she considered pleasant and mannerly, Flora became curious what kind of men frequented the hotel. The Texaco filling station was down the street from the hotel, and one evening she was talking with the owner as he filled her gas tank. "I've seen the other end of this and I've wondered what sort of men go to those women," Flora remarked. The station owner laughed. "You'd be surprised. Next time you're at the station and I see one of them, I'll nod my head."

The owner did just that the next time Flora was at the pump, and she was startled when she followed the nod and saw an out-of-town man who drove a Cadillac and wore rings with large diamonds in them. This certainly did not fit her stereotype. She had not expected Dell's customers to be so polished and obviously wealthy.

It was nearing Thanksgiving in mid 1960, and Dell was apparently having trouble making a choice at the meat counter in the Safeway grocery store. Salesgirl Beverly Bonsell walked up to her. "Could I help you?"

"I was wondering which is the best turkey."

"The Butterball Turkey is probably best because it's the most expensive. But I always get one of the less expensive ones," Beverly explained, thinking about her own need to be thrifty.

Dell said, "Thanks," and picked up a Butterball.

Several months later, when Beverly's husband finished repairs at Dell's country place, she handed him an extra $10. "Here, give this to your wife so she can get a turkey."

He took the money home to Beverly. "How come you told Dell Burke we couldn't afford a turkey?"

Beverly was surprised. "I guess I did, but I didn't mean to."

Tax time rolled around with relentless regularity even at the Yellow Hotel. As usual the accountant called Dell to let her know when he would be in town, and she began to make her list. There were always so many details she could use his help with—details she chose not to share with anyone else.

Each visit called for an accounting of her bank deposit box. "Dell, I want you to stop putting cash in that box," he said each time.

"You're right. I shouldn't leave that much cash in there." However, the next visit revealed little change in this habit, perhaps left over from times when banks failed.

They sat at the kitchen table sipping coffee. He could see that the hotel was not being kept up as neatly as it had been before. "Want me to get rid of those newspapers?" He pointed at the pile in one corner.

"Oh, would you? Thanks."

"How about those boxes on top of them?"

"Those came from the Denver May Company yesterday. I haven't had time to go through them. You could carry them upstairs for me. Thanks."

With a calculating look, Dell asked, "What do you know about ranch prices?"

"Why do you ask?"

"I'm thinking I might sell my country place. I don't go out there much . . . "

"I could ask around."

"Do that," she said with such a sly smile he suspected she was looking more for his reaction than for a buyer.

The tax computation went smoothly. Generally, Dell kept clear records, easy to work with.

"Anything else I can do for you?" he asked as he was folding up the last of the paperwork.

"Would you mind taking me over to the grocery store? These poor animals are running out of food." She patted the little Pekingese beside her, who was keeping a wary eye on the visitor. He did not like men, and sometimes snapped at them.

Dell went in the store alone. "This won't take long, and it'll look better if you stay in the car."

As Dell lingered by the vegetables, Polly Boner stopped to chat. "How are you today, Dell?"

"I'm fine. I just needed some cat food for those poor hungry cats that hanging around the back door."

On the way back to the hotel, the accountant remembered something. "Several guys at the office want to meet you. Any chance you could visit with them next weekend?"

She considered it for a moment and nodded. "Yes, Sunday evening would be fine. Bring them by about seven o'clock."

She met them at the front door, dressed attractively, with the right dash of perfume. She ushered them into the parlor and asked, "Would you like a glass of Wild Turkey?" Assured this was acceptable, she served each of them one glass. She asked all sorts of questions: where they went to school, where they came from originally, what their families did for a living. She firmly informed them that while they were welcome as visitors, she would end their work with her if they chose to visit her girls. A gracious hostess, she was flattered by their interest.

After they left, she sat down to look at the summary of her year's expenses. She had subscribed to a number of magazines, including those about fashion, women's interests, business, and investment, along with local newspapers. "Makes good reading on long quiet nights," she said, patting the dog beside her. "And then there's the companies I invested in," she went on. Yen cocked his head, as though he understood. "Some paid off, and some were just a lark. I like to support local ones, but the national companies usually pay better. It's been fun." She pulled him onto her lap. "And I've done fairly well with the mining, beverage producers, utilities, and all sorts of others. Bet folks in this town would be surprised if they knew . . . anyway, I guess it's better they don't."

Baby doll pajamas were the rage in 1967, and they looked attractive on a trim young body. The girls from Dell's hotel surrounded the table at Whiteaker's store looking through the assortment. Don watched with amusement from a distance, until one girl finally motioned him over to them. "How much for these?"

"Those run about $5, maybe $10. Want to see the special ones?"

"Sure."

He brought out pretty ones with piping down the middle.

The girls were clearly pleased, but seemed a little uneasy. Finally one admitted, "We wouldn't be able to get them open easily. They're closed; they won't come off fast enough."

Don got creative. "If I can fix that opening, are you interested?"

"Sure," the girls chorused.

He went in the back of the store, got out scissors, sheared along the piping so that they'd open, and sold half a dozen at double the price of the ordinary ones. The girls thanked him and reached into their bras for the cash. They counted out the bills and handed them to him.

It was Saturday afternoon at Whiteaker's Store. When two men selected items they were considering for purchase, Don nodded toward the changing rooms, and said, "Those are empty." Assuming different styles, one chose a tailored look and the other a more casual approach. Both picked up new socks, new underwear, new shirts, and new pants. A bandanna on sale was added to their piles. When they stepped out in their new attire, Don told them, "Boy, don't you look spiffy. Where're you going tonight?"

"Oh, we're gonna go see Dell," replied the one. "Yeah, that's the best place in town for a drink," added the other. Along with a number of the other country men, who were also dressed in clean new clothes, they found good conversations, a few drinks, good companionship, and sometimes good sex at the Yellow Hotel.

Darkness only added to the excitement of "trick or treating" at Halloween. Few lights shone on First Street where the Yellow Hotel stood. Denis Peterson and his brother decided to include the hotel on their route. "Remember you won't get candy here," his brother warned nine-year-old Denis. "She just gives money."

Dell met them at the front door. "I don't have any candy, but wait a minute." Shortly, she was back with a small roll of bills from which she pulled one for each child. "When you get older, come back and see us."

Several years later, a little girl knocked at Dell's door hoping for a handful of fabled candy or money, only to hear, "I don't have anything, but come back and see us when you grow up." Later, the children and their families wondered whether Dell was keeping an eye out for girls to employ and boys who could become customers when they got older.

In 1967 James E. "Jim" Barrett accepted Governor Hathaway's appointment for attorney general of Wyoming. Shortly after the appointment, he was tidying up the loose ends of his law practice to leave for Cheyenne when Dell called. "I've gone over my assets with that accountant you suggested."

"The one with Raab, Raush, and Gaymon?"

"Yes, and I'd like to draw up a new will," she informed him. "I'd like to have your help. When would be convenient?"

He said, "Oh, any time."

"Are you in your office Saturday?"

"I usually don't see people then because I do paperwork."

"Good," she said. "Let's get together next Saturday."

They discussed the will carefully. He went over the procedure of getting two witnesses and other details. On the following Monday he dictated the will and mailed it to her. Since he was leaving Lusk, he did not keep an office copy. Before long, she inserted new items and omitted others. Later, the CPA working on Dell's estate discovered that will. She had never finalized it.

As always, she used her personal name with her family. During their 1967 visit, Marie gave Roy and Phyllis Fisher a Wyoming commemorative plate that began a family collection of commemoratives. She also gave Roy a whiskey bottle from the Wyoming Bicentennial. In a move that surprised the Fisher family and caused Loraine to note that her great-aunt "would turn a buck" when she could, about six months later Marie asked him to return it. "I can get $50 for that bottle." Although he liked it, he sent it back.

Just in time for Christmas 1967, Dell gave herself a gift. "Look what I got," she told a friend. She pulled the new vacuum sweeper from the box from Rainbow Sales and Service. "Even after trading in my old one, this thing cost an arm and a leg. It was $378."

"Better last a long time," the friend noted.

"It will," she said determinedly. "Now I can get in those dirty corners and keep this place clean."

Keeping the hotel and country place house tidy was becoming harder for seventy-nine-year-old Dell. It took more effort to make beds and do laundry. She looked around the kitchen as she sipped her morning coffee. Floors were harder to reach. She picked up the bowls in which she fed the cats and Yen. Scraping at the dried food on the sides, she added a new layer for the hungry mouths.

Dell's Pekingese, Yen Chee, was increasingly in need of veterinary attention. Trips to the vet in Casper provided an opportunity to get out of town for the day and eat out as well.

Roger and Beverly Bonsell, who were neighbors to Dell, did various tasks for her at the hotel and at the country place. She had begun to turn to Roger for trips to Casper. "Yen's not well. Think you could take us to Casper tomorrow?" she asked him on the phone one night. Roger agreed and the next day after Dr. Popish saw Yen, Dell turned to Roger. "We're done. Let's go get pancakes." One of her favorite places was the Pancake House.

Appropriately sexy clothing was not always easy to find in Lusk, and Dell was pleased to discover that Amy Andrews was a capable and conscientious seamstress. One day a pretty blond girl squirmed as Amy set another pin in place. "Hold still," the seamstress said as she adjusted the skirt. "I don't want to stick you." The miniskirt and bolero of fake leopard fur would soon become part of the girl's costumes.

"Eva, you sit quiet," Amy warned her young daughter, who was admiring the beautiful beaded lamp on a nearby table. The hotel's room was crowded with interesting things. Dolls lined the shelves.

Dell visited while Amy worked. "I've always wanted a sewing machine. What kind would you recommend?" she asked Amy.

"I like Singer," Amy said, describing what she could do with hers.

Amy was surprised to learn that not all customers went to the hotel. "Most of them do," Dell explained, "but during hunting season, I usually take large groups out to the country place. It's more private that way. The girls go out, too."

Several more times, Amy went to the hotel to measure, fit, or alter clothing for the girls, each time looking for ways to tend to her own children. It became cumbersome, and she offered a solution. "If it's convenient, come over to my house," she told the girl after her skirt was fitted. "Then I don't have to worry about my kids."

The girl was surprised. "You want us to come to your house?"

"Everybody comes to my house."

"This is the first time I've had an invitation to someone's home." The girl seemed genuinely touched.

Before they arrived, Amy laid down the rules to her children. "Now you treat them like you do anybody else. Be nice to these people. They're just doing their job."

That afternoon, as the kids sat around watching, one girl turned to Eva. "What grade are you in? You know, it's really important for you to stay in school and get good grades." She seemed genuinely curious and soon had the children engaged in conversation so interesting they almost forgot who the girl was.

As the girls left, they paid their bill and laid a tip in Amy's hand. "That's too much."

"No, you deserve this. Thank you so much."

Later, Amy took her family grocery shopping. Young Eva saw Dell standing beside the meat counter and ran up to her.

Quietly, Dell told the child, "You really shouldn't talk to me here."

Eva was confused. She had talked with Dell at the hotel, so it was hard to understand.

Amy's husband did repair and maintenance at his shop. When Amy worked at the hotel, his friends liked to tease him. "I see your wife's working for Dell again."

"Yeah, she said she was working there today. "Course, I'll be over there at the hotel myself tomorrow."

After he had the washing machine working again, Dell led Joe into the kitchen. "Would you like tea? Or would you rather have coffee?"

"Coffee would taste real good."

"Have some cookies. Colette made them this morning." A plateful of cookies sat waiting on the table.

She turned the conversation back to the hotel. "Could you come out next week and look at the drier? It doesn't seem to get hot enough."

"Sure, give me a call and we'll set a time."

In February 1968 Dell wrote a check to Singer Sewing Company for $222.75 for the machine she had coveted.

People who worked for Dell, people who served her, even people who frequented her hotel became her friends. When her dry cleaning lady became ill, Dell took her soup and visited her daily until she could tend to her household again herself.

Dell stayed in touch with many of the girls who had worked for her, providing money when they were in trouble and sending toys and clothing for their children. She enjoyed buying gifts for them.

In the 1960s the Lusk Chamber of Commerce placed signs to advertise Lusk businesses along the highways leading into town. The chamber paid the sign fee for Wyoming, Nebraska, and Colorado. Members bought their own signs for $300. Soon signs for Coffee Cup, Ranger Hotel, Midwest Hardware, XL Café, Gamble's Hardware, Covered Wagon, Quality Shop, Dell's Hotel, and a number of others were erected. The slogan on the sign for the Yellow Hotel read:

STOP AT LUSK WYOMING

YOU'RE ON AN (SIC) HISTORIC ROUTE

DELL'S HOTEL

In 1965 Dell purchased a somewhat different sign from the Star Brite Signs company in Ft. Collins. It read:

SMILE

YOU'LL BE IN LUSK

BY DARK!

DELL'S HOTEL

Dell had joined the Lusk Chamber of Commerce in the 1950s, and she remained a member through 1980. Although she supported it annually, Dell never attended a chamber meeting. Once more her financial support was felt but not seen.

In the spring of 1969, Bruce Bergstrom was a twenty-seven-year-old "rookie" at Raab, Rausch, and Gaymon in Cheyenne, a recent college graduate after two years in the army. He accompanied E. O. Davis to Lusk to handle tax affairs for local ranchers and businessmen. They were sorting through paperwork in the Ranger Hotel when Dell called E. O., who explained he was busy but his associate was available. Reluctantly, Dell agreed to meet Bruce. The men dropped everything and within minutes were at the back door of the Yellow Hotel. Dell ushered them into a small room and served beer while they talked. Dell asked about Bruce's aspirations, whether he was married, if he wanted to have children. Their conversation consisted of trading questions wherein she learned a great deal about this potential employee. She must have approved of him as she requested that his services begin.

The next morning, Bruce appeared at the Yellow Hotel for his first appointment. Dell wore a purple pantsuit and smelled very good. Automatically using the manners he used with his grandmother, he slid his arm through hers and she stood tall as they walked to the bank. They passed local people on the sidewalk, many of whom said, "Hello,

Dell." She smiled and said, "Good day," to each one.

Later, Bruce learned her behavior that day was in sharp contrast with her usual reticence. Perhaps Dell was enjoying the role of Grande Dame as they walked arm in arm along the street.

At the bank she requested her safe deposit box. "Let's inventory the contents, Bruce." Although he suspected this was "make work" to check him out, he complied. For the next several years, Dell called on Bruce when she wanted help with accounting and other work.

"Come post NO HUNTING signs for me." Bruce purchased about forty-five signs from the hardware store and posted them all over the country place. "I need a package taken to Cheyenne." It was a striking photograph of Dell as a young woman that she wanted reproduced and colored. Bruce wanted a copy, but the photographer said a copy would cost over $100. Another call: "I need Bruce to come for two weeks." At the rate of $8 to $10 per hour, the firm was pleased to send him. He spent the entire time inventorying phonograph records at her country place.

Entering the country house for the first time, Bruce felt as though he had walked into a time warp. The interior decor was pink and green with art deco furnishings of the 1940s.

The morning after he arrived, Dell brought out breakfast. She held a bag from Safeway in her arms as she asked, "Do you like pickled artichokes?"

"Yes, I do, Dell," he said, wondering to himself, "What the hell are artichokes?"

"So do I. I just love them. I've brought you a couple of jars." That was breakfast that day.

The jukebox was in the basement along with several hundred

records. Every so often, Dell or her girl Lisa visited him. Dell had made it clear that there was to be no patronizing of her establishment if Bruce wished to remain her accountant. When Dell visited in the evening, they sat in the stillness of dusk, surrounded by the hum of mosquitoes, and she talked about her years in the Yukon. She said that she hated and distrusted Canadians, and she described the years she spent at Convent School in Grand Forks, North Dakota, whose mother superior she referred to as the head madam.

Dell was proud of the Charlie Russell picture in the hotel front room that a patron had given to her. Although she was sure it was an original, Bruce risked their relationship with his doubts. He showed her a book containing Russell pictures, but it was neither returned nor further discussed.

On the kitchen windowsill of the country house sat a box of rocks and arrowheads from her garden. Bruce asked permission to look for other artifacts. She assured him, "Keep anything you find out there." He found three arrowheads and a number of chips. In anthills beside the house, there were so many beads he wondered if a burial site might be nearby.

Over the next several years Dell and Bruce became good friends. He enjoyed the stories she liked to tell of her early years in Alaska and Montana, and she appreciated his adulation and interest. He willingly gave her a helping hand.

Fisher family news was always interesting. Dell sipped her coffee as she read about a Rupp family reunion from her cousin Myrtle's letter of September 1969 sent from Sheridan, Wyoming. After visiting the family, Myrtle had stopped at the cemetery in Rolette, North Dakota, to see the family graves. Dell sighed. It had been a long time since she had been home, and she was glad to hear that the tombstones were standing solidly and the grounds were well kept. She knew her mother had wanted that. She thought about the shelterbelt Jerry had planted along the edge of their country place with Roy's help, and she smiled as she read that ranchers in North Dakota were planting them between Rolette and Rugby. Jerry had been right to plant that line of trees.

The family news in October 1969 was not as pleasant. The disappearance of her favorite brother had been hard forty-seven years before, and now the death of his sixty-three-year-old son, Roy Traver Fisher, was almost as hard.

In the years that followed, Dell was pleased that Roy's wife, Phyllis, and daughter, Loraine, still stopped at the hotel to see her on their visits with friends in Nebraska.

Dell looked down at the cats eating from tins of the floor in her hotel kitchen. Since Jerry died, nothing seemed to matter as much. She wished he were there to talk to once more. Talk about her family and their visits and problems. About their investments. About Amy and the sewing she did so well. She couldn't help wondering what he would have thought about Bruce. Well, it didn't matter much now. It was time to go upstairs to check the rooms and make sure everything was in order for the evening, and then it would be business as usual. Again.

The End of an Era, 1970–1980

Bruce Bergstrom knocked on the hotel's back door. "Tax time," he called, sticking his head inside as he tapped crusty snow from his shoes.

Dell stepped into the hallway and called out, "C'mon in. Have some coffee to warm you up."

Her living room was piled with papers, but Dell kept good records, and it was easy to put them in order for the IRS. They discussed some of the papers as they organized them.

"That's where I paid for those chamber of commerce signs through this summer. I wonder if I should keep that up."

"People notice those signs and ask about your hotel."

"They're paying off, then."

Dell's girl Lisa stepped into the room. "Staying for dinner, Bruce?"

"Of course, he is." Dell turned to him. "You are, aren't you?"

The tantalizing odor of Italian cooking seeped into the room. His mouth watered. "You twisted my arm. I'd be pleased to have dinner with you ladies."

Dinner conversation ranged across topics Bruce had heard before. "I don't know how those guys do it. They talk against me from the pulpit, then ask if the coast is clear to see Lisa." Dell shook her head as she dove into both the spaghetti and a favorite diatribe.

"I saw hypocrisy in that North Dakota Convent years ago, and I see it here. Doesn't matter which church they attend on Sunday, or what they say about me, they come here during the week. Such hypocrites." Dell was disgusted. Bruce had learned not to disagree or agree with her on some subjects. Soon the topic turned to politicians. While Dell had worked with them over the years and appreciated their efforts, she still could not stomach their manipulations. "Especially that governor we have. I just can't stand him."

"But, Dell, after all," Lisa said with a grin, "he's just a man."

"I know! And men aren't . . . " Dell glanced at Bruce. "You're an exception . . . never mind."

"Your taxes are nearly done," Bruce said, hoping to turn the conversation. "Anything else you need?"

"Not this time. I'll call you."

Bruce smiled and had another helping of spaghetti.

At the south end of Lusk, the Fireside Restaurant served good food in a pleasant atmosphere. This made it a good meeting place when a newcomer came to work for Dell. "It's quiet now, but we'll have more business during hunting season," Dell told the new girl over dinner. "Tricia, you'll like it here. Tips are good even when business isn't brisk."

The girl nodded and asked, "Any other girls?"

"Lisa's back from Vegas for the winter." Dell went on. "Remember that even though you may become friends with your customers, never speak to them in public." Dell leaned her auburn head close to the girl. "*Never* speak to them in public."

"What happens if I do?"

"Let me tell you a story," began the legendary raconteur. "A couple years ago, a pretty girl I'll call Jane worked for me. She was good. She made men happy. But it was not enough." Dell shook head. "I warned her, like I'm warning you, not to talk to people outside the hotel."

"What happened?" asked Tricia.

"Jane and another girl went to the Coffee Cup. They were sitting there when one of Jane's favorite customers came in. She looked up and said, 'Well, hi there!' and called him by name. When she noticed his wife, she smiled at her, too. The woman was shocked. Jane didn't mention it when she got back to the hotel, but I'd already heard."

Tricia was listening carefully as Dell continued. "Jane and her suitcase were on the next bus out of town before she could say a thing. And that's what happens."

"Not to worry, Dell. I keep my mouth shut. Business is business and personal is personal. My boyfriend would get me if I mixed those two."

"Good. Then, we understand each other?"

Tricia nodded. "By the way, I noticed a telephone. Can I use it?"

"You're welcome to, but if it's long distance, make the calls collect."

Later, while Lisa and Dell were busy, Tricia picked up the phone. "Number please," came the familiar request.

Softly she said, "I want to call Menominee, Wisconsin, collect," and gave the number. She carefully spelled out the name, adding, "I don't want my family to know where I'm calling from. Can you manage that?"

"Sure," replied the operator. "I can just tell them they have a collect call from Lusk, Wyoming. Do they know you're here?"

"They do. Thanks."

The operator thought how sad that was.

In September 1970, Governor Stan Hathaway appointed Jim Griffith the next Wyoming state treasurer, and Dell's longtime friend left his job as editor of the *Lusk Herald* for Cheyenne. Once more, one of her local confidants moved into the state political scene. Yes, she did have "friends in high places," and while she was pleased for his political rise, she would miss their frequent conversations over a cup of coffee.

Business was down in Lusk, but the hotel continued to pull in hunters from across the country. Dell placed ads in the hunting magazines inviting hunters to come relax at the Yellow Hotel. It worked, as evidenced by a letter Dell wrote to her CPA, Bruce Bergstrom, on November 1, 1970: "I was glad to hear from you. I lost your home address. Please give it to me. I have been real busy. Goofy hunters, etc. I sure need a rest away from people. They should have a bounty on politicians. I had four hunters on my place looking for antelope." The letter ended with an invitation to visit soon.

When Bruce arrived in January to do the taxes, Dell was ready for him. "The papers are in here, " she said, waving toward the bedroom. "Don't mind the clutter. Lisa and I'll clean it up before she leaves for Vegas." He noticed the bedroom was worse than usual. Numerous bottles and jars of perfume and cosmetics sat on the dresser. Clothes were tightly jammed in the built-in closet, and a few garish colors struck his eyes. "Here's the rest." She handed him a stack of papers. "You can work on them in here."

As he began, he realized that she was nosing around in the

closet. After a while, she pulled out a piece of newspaper tied with a string. "You've talked about that old Packard I have. Would you like to have this?" She held out a 1937–1938 Packard hood ornament from one of her old cars.

"Would I? May I?" Bruce was delighted. She was a Packard fan, and he was an old car aficionado. "What a treasure."

She laughed. "I don't need it anymore. Oh hey, want some old stock certificates? They aren't any good."

"Sure, I collect paper memorabilia. Thanks, Dell."

She pulled out several certificates from Piggly Wiggly Food Stores and Durant Motor Co.

After the taxes were done, she asked, "Would you mind running me over to Casper? Yen is sick again, and Dr. Popish is the best vet I know."

"Just let me call the firm first."

As usual, Bruce drove her Chrysler while Dell tenderly tucked Yen into her lap under his blanket. Every so often the dog shivered.

"How are things going with you, Bruce?"

"Just fine. I told you about Barbara, didn't I?"

"Yes, how is she?"

"She's fine. We've set a date."

"You have? Already?"

"We'll be married in August." He could sense her displeasure.

"At least she's not Canadian. Those people are hard to live with. They try to control everything, and tell you what to do all the time." She thought for a moment. "You do know there are ways to control things, don't you?"

Bruce knew what was coming and wished he could change the

subject, but as usual, it was impossible. All the way to Casper, no matter what he said, the conversation veered back to the subject of too many unwanted children in the world and the need for population control.

"Do you want to have children?"

"I haven't really thought about it."

"You need to think about it. Have you considered sterilization?"

He glanced sideways at her. Her tiny Pekingese was tucked inside a blanket marked Yen Chee. This was her child. "No, I haven't considered sterilization, but I'll think about it."

Subsequent visits always included a discourse on world population, sterilization, and population control. Dell had definite ideas on these topics and voiced her opinions strongly to Bruce.

In 1971 Loraine along with her mother, Phyllis, visited her great-aunt at her country place. They had realized that she was the last surviving member of Roy Traver Fisher's family, and they wanted to maintain contact as long as possible. In April of the same year, Lusk Attorney James E. Barrett was sworn in as circuit judge. With satisfaction, Dell read the newspaper article describing her friend's rise in position.

The last of the snow finally melted off, and signs of spring were abundant. Tiny lettuce-green buds topped the trees, and crocuses and daffodils held up brightly colored blossoms across town. Bruce and Barbara would be married in August, and Dell had been inviting them to come visit. One day Bruce pulled his car up behind the hotel, and Dell met him at the back door. She peered around his shoulder. "Who's in the car?"

"Barbara."

She said, "Well, get her in here."

She yelled into the hotel, "Lisa, Lisa! Look who's here. Bruce Bergstrom's here." Lisa joined them in the kitchen. While they caught up on the news, Dell fed tidbits to her dog.

Lisa waved her hand at the food scraps and dirty dishes on the table and sink. Papers were all over the floor. "Sorry for the mess. I'm getting ready to head back to Las Vegas, but I'll be back when Camp Guernsey opens this summer."

As they talked, Dell leaned over toward Barbara. "Would you like to come work for me, dear?" After a pregnant pause during which Barbara could only breathe deeply, Dell went on, "I'd like to find a chauffeur." The tension dropped as Barbara declined with a smile.

Despite her concerns about overpopulation, Dell accepted that Bruce and Barbara wanted a family. On her Christmas card in 1974, she wrote that she was looking forward to seeing them and asked about their baby.

Bruce received several more calls to take Dell and Yen Chee to Casper. Neighbors and other townspeople provided transportation, too. On January 5, 1972, Yen Chee died. The next day, Dell wrote Bruce: "We have had the coldest weather in years with six inches of snow. Yen died yesterday in Popish Clinic in Casper. I sent him up there Tuesday. They called me yesterday; they could not do anything for him as the eye and jaw was (sic) malignant and advised putting him to sleep. It was the toughest decision I ever decided (sic) on. I hope I did right. I sure miss him."

Lisa put her arms around Dell as she finished the letter to Bruce. "Deciding to let them put Yen to sleep was like telling the doctor to kill your baby." Tears snuck down Dell's cheek as she sipped her tea.

"Where's he now?" Lisa asked softly.

"They buried him near the clinic." Dell sighed. "I still have his blanket. I guess I'll keep it. When I can, I'll go back to the clinic and put up a small stone."

They sat in silence for a time, marked by an occasional sniffle. Lisa smiled. "You like animals so much. Like they're your children." She glanced around at the food pans where feline heads gathered.

"Yes, they're like children."

It was a small thing, but she still had to smile as she read the letter. She knew Jerry would have appreciated the recognition for the shelterbelt they had planted at the back edge of the country place. She turned the check for $86.33 over in her hand before rereading the words from the U.S. Department of Agriculture, Niobrara County ASC Committee in Lusk: "This is for Agriculture Conservation Program REAP practices on which you have requested Federal cost-sharing under the 1972 program. You are to be commended on the conservation practices which you are carrying out on your farm or ranch . . . "

Stan Hahn, son of the owners of Gamble's store had been raised in Lusk where he and his friends were aware of the activities at the Yellow Hotel. Not many years before, the Texaco Station down the street from the hotel had been the vantage point from which he and high-school friends had giggled and watched cars with families approach the hotel for lodging only to be turned away. One time, his friends were selling magazines door to door. They hoped for a peek at the girls in the Yellow Hotel, but Dell blocked the door and firmly told them she was not interested. In the 1970s Stan was working at the Texaco Station, and today the hotel owner was a customer. "Could someone come fix my tire?" Dell asked when she telephoned the station.

Stan was elected. At the country place, he discovered Dell had turned too sharply in the parking lot and rolled a front tire off the rim. He attached the spare tire so she could drive the Chrysler into town, where they could put the tire back on the rim. While he worked, Dell stood nearby. "This car has quite a few miles on it, but it's still really good," Dell commented.

"You've kept it in good shape."

"You know, some kids wanted to buy it because it has a hemi engine."

His ears perked up. "Want to sell it?"

She laughed. "No. It was fun to talk about it though."

On one Halloween night in the mid-1970s, the crisp fall evening was perfect for haunting. Leaves covered the ground and mild temperatures invited outdoor activity.

"Ready for Halloween?" Lisa asked Dell.

"I think so . . . we've got plenty of candy this year and bubble gum too."

"Need help handing it out?" asked Tricia, hopefully.

"Sure, the candy's in a bowl on the little table by the door. We'll all go."

A knock at the front door drew them down the hall. When they opened the door, two tall masked people dressed in costumes sang out, "Trick or treat," and began giggling.

At first, Dell could not tell who they were, except they were adult women. Then she recognized her neighbors' voices and laughingly handed out strings of bubble gum.

The rest of their visitors were much smaller, usually holding out open bags even before calling out the greeting. The evening went by quickly.

Suddenly there was a loud thud at the side of the hotel. Tricia jumped. "What was that?"

"I don't know. Turn off the lights." In the dim streetlight outside, they could make out the shapes of several boys huddled together. "I don't recognize them, but here they come again," Dell said softly.

Another thud and a long scratching sound raked the long side of the building. Young masculine giggles could be heard. More unidentifiable noises followed.

"Want to call the police?" Lisa was concerned.

"No, let's wait. Maybe they'll just go away." They watched the boys inch their way up onto the porch, and the women held their breath while there was a loud knocking on the door before the boys ran down the steps.

Inspection the next morning revealed no damage. "No new paint job this year," Dell said with a sigh of relief. "Some years, they spray paint or smear awful stuff on the walls, and it takes a new coat of yellow paint to clean it up."

Informing potential customers that the hotel was in business was always a challenge. In the 1970s Dell discovered another magazine that would carry her ad. In March 1973 she sent a check for $25 marked "for advertising" to the Wyoming Peace Officers Association (Wyoming Peace Officer Magazine Fund).

Dell was a private person, yet in 1973 she allowed Charles Hillinger of the *Los Angeles Times* to interview her. How it came about is unknown, but some of her history was revealed in the March 26 edition of the California newspaper. The story appeared in other papers, including one in Nebraska and the *Arizona Republic* in Phoenix.

A gifted storyteller, Dell may have embellished events and changed details. She gave a good performance for the journalist to record—and for the world to read. The interview was held in the mahogany-paneled living room of the Yellow Hotel, a room filled with paintings—including the ones by Charlie Russell and Broken Rope. Pictures of cowboys, Indians, and the Old West decorated the walls. The article described Dell's generosity in helping scores of people down on their luck during the Depression as well as her single-handedly floating a water-sewer-and-light bond.

Hillinger quoted Dell as saying, "I sent two boys through college, one through Stanford, the other UCLA. They both got Ph.D.s. Every Christmas they send me cards thanking me. Their families believed the boys were educated on scholarships. Wouldn't they be surprised if they knew who it was that gave the scholarships?"

At the same time, Hillinger noted she was still not an accepted part of the local scene. "They all know me," said Dell with a touch of sadness in her husky voice. "But all they do is nod and smile."

Hillinger admitted he could not get Dell to tell her age and described her as a trim five-foot three-inch redhead "with not a speck of gray showing" who had to be at least seventy-five. His comments probably amused the eighty-five-year-old madam with freshly colored hair. This interview produced several oft-quoted phrases she has been credited with. "I came to Lusk with the oil boom here. I believed the name of the place was Lust." "Before I came here I made good money as a call girl in Butte and before that in Juneau. I made $10,000 one year in Juneau." "I wouldn't trade my life for anything. I'm glad of it.

I've made a lot of money. Traveled the world. For me it's been a good life. I've met some of the best. Governors. Senators." The only regret she mentioned was that she had never had children of her own.

Hillinger noted that Dell had come to Lusk when it was a wide-open frontier town with an economy based on oil booms and had operated the "sporting house" through it all.

His article went on: "When this place was booming, money was plentiful, so were women, booze and gambling."

Dell claimed that while prostitution was illegal, no one had ever threatened to shut her down, adding, "Maybe it's because I know too much for everybody's good. There are ten churches in town. But not a minister or a priest has ever preached against me so far as I know. And I've known them all on first-name basis. Like the movie, it has always been 'never on Sunday' at the Yellow Hotel. That's so none of the boys come here instead of going to church. I certainly wouldn't want any of my girls competing."

The interview was widely read and added considerably to the mystique around the Yellow Hotel Madam, at home and across the nation.

In the early 1970s a heavy late winter snowstorm clogged the roads and made it difficult to read the city electric meters. As the meter reader stood reading the meter at the Yellow Hotel, Dell stuck her head out the door, and asked, "Hey, take me out to my country place so I can feed my cats?"

He protested, "Sorry, Dell, I'm on 'city time.'"

"Oh, pooh! Those cats're gonna starve. You've gotta take me out. Please."

She begged so hard, he finally decided to take her out to her country place rather than make an enemy out of her.

The Fisher family visit in 1974 was special. Loraine and Phyllis had reservations to visit Grand Teton National Park on the far western side of Wyoming. Before they left for their trip, they shared many memories with Marie over dinner at the country place—memories of earlier visits and her life in the Dakotas. When they returned, Marie listened intently as they told about their travels. It was a memorable trip. In the mountains, Phyllis and Loraine had located a stable where they rode horses and took a trail ride. "You know, I've always wanted to do that," Marie said as she pointed a piece of steak on her fork at Phyllis. "Wish I was younger and I'd have joined you." Too soon her visitors were on their way once more. But they had promised to come back.

Dell's weekly visits to Kut and Kurl were an opportunity to visit with her hairdresser, Della Clarke, while she had her hair shampooed and set. She enjoyed talking with other patrons, such as Polly Boner. After *The Happy Hooker* was published in 1972, Polly wondered what Dell thought of it. "Have you read *The Happy Hooker*?" she asked Dell.

Dell's quick response was "Yes. It's a terrible book. Those people did all those things and wrote about it. That's disgusting."

Polly often gave Dell a ride home. She noticed how badly Dell needed to have her teeth fixed, but she didn't dare ask why Dell neglected them. The question would have been too personal. Since Dell didn't drive anymore, Polly told her to call if she needed to get groceries or anything else. Dell agreed and from time to time took Polly up on the offer. Whether Polly had planned to shop or not, she said yes, and invited Dell to go along.

Dell's grocery cart was always stacked with cans of cat food, cans of food for herself, meat for the freezer, tea, and other items.

Appreciative cats swarmed around Polly and Dell as they delivered the food to the hotel kitchen.

As summer days dragged by long and dry, Dell became concerned about how the lack of rain would affect the ranchers. One day at Kut and Kurl, she took matters into her own hands. "All right, everybody. Let's do a rain dance, and see if we can't bring rain," Dell called out. She stood up in the middle of the beauty shop, dancing and chanting. Reminiscent of the rain dances performed by local actors during the annual "Legend of the Rawhide Buttes" presentation in Lusk, other patrons joined her.

After the beautician finished setting her hair, Dell leaned over to her and said quietly, "Would you come over by the hotel when you get off work?"

The beautician was surprised but agreed to stop by. Later that day she arrived at the hotel, and Dell led her into the kitchen. A large box containing various kinds of cheese sat on the table. "I receive one of these every so often, and I really don't care for them. Would you like this?"

"Why, sure."

"Good. It's brand-new. Hasn't been opened."

The two women visited for a time. As they sipped their coffee, Dell began to talk about the old days at the country place. She told about visits from her relatives and how she always had them out to the country place. She described the wonderful parties she had held out there and the way she had decorated the house.

Dell enjoyed wearing beautiful clothing, although she rarely did so in Lusk. Her mink coat was stored at Neusteters in Denver, where she could wear it while she was there.

Dell had eagerly awaited the arrival of her new kitchen appliance, and she was pleased to see the Gamble's store truck pull up behind the hotel. Store owner Merle Hahn lifted the box carefully from the truck bed and carried it to the back door.

She held the door open. "Please take it in the kitchen. The old oven stopped working last week, and I'm hoping this will last a long time." Dell watched him pull the gleaming new microwave-convection oven from the box and then asked, "Want a cup of coffee?"

"Sure."

"And then you can show me how it works," she commanded.

Merle took his time, explaining all the features. All the while, Dell kept up a stream of conversation, about the weather, about ranching, about furniture she might want to buy, about how the new oven would be used, until he finally said, "Well, Dell, I gotta get back to the store to relieve Phyllis for lunch." He could tell she was lonely, but he had work to do.

Most bank employees liked having Dell and her girls come in. As soon as they walked in, the tellers appreciatively inhaled the aroma of good perfume. Money left in the vault overnight provided a fragrant pleasure as the money was counted the next morning. Some tellers tried to keep part of the money in the vault so the lovely odor would last.

Rumors that Dell Burke wanted to sell the country place must have circulated from time to time throughout Lusk because a number of people approached her over the years. By the mid-1970s, she spent most of her time in town at the hotel. That's where she was, sitting in her living room, when Bill and Hester Smith came by one day.

After exchanging pleasantries, Bill commented, "I hear you're thinking of selling your country place."

"Now where did you hear that?" Dell's eyes twinkled.

"I don't exactly remember." Bill dodged the question.

They continued to discuss what would be involved for Dell if she sold the country place, what she would gain and what she might lose. Finally, she said, "Bill, I'm not sure I want to sell any property yet, but I'll keep you in mind. Thanks for coming over."

It might have been about then that the Petersons became interested in the property. However, no matter how reasonable the presentation was, Dell did not want to sell.

"You're getting on up in years, Dell. You won't be moving back out there and putting the land to work."

"I know," she admitted, "but I guess I just want to keep it."

Harry Brown approached her with the possibility of purchasing the country place, only to hear her say, "No. That's not anything I want to do. That place means a lot to me."

Jerry's rock-encrusted crocks still adorned the patio where he had left them, and there were so many memories that haunted the place. Parties they had held. Barbecues. Business she had done there. Weekends with the girls. Times with Jerry. She wasn't ready to let it go.

Business was slow some mornings at the Whiteaker store, and owner Don Whteaker took advantage of that time to visit with other businesspeople along the street. As he approached the back door of the hotel, Dell called out, "C'mon in," and waved him into the kitchen. Sitting down for his usual cup of coffee, he began describing the latest sales promotions, new businesses opening up, old businesses that were closing, and whatever else he thought she would be interested in.

Suddenly Dell leaned over and asked hesitantly, "Heard anyone gossip about me?"

"Nah, I haven't," Don answered. Even if he had, he would have chosen not to share it. Dell was in her eighties. Why should he upset her by reporting gossip? "You stay pretty much here at the hotel now, don't you?"

"Sometimes I go out to the country place for a few days, but mostly I'm in here." She seemed to draw into herself. "There's just bad people out there. And they're after me, and after me."

Don repeated, "Well, yeah, there's some bad people out there, but I don't think they're after you."

Generally, during those later years, with the exception of Camp Guernsey Days and hunting season, Dell spent most of her time alone or with her one remaining girl and companion, Lisa. Occasional cowboys, travelers, and others stopped by. During "busy" seasons, she recruited a girl from Denver, Hot Springs, or wherever she could find one.

Just before hunting season, Dell ran into a lady who had worked for her a couple years before. She walked up to her in the post office and said loudly, "I need you to come over and work." Bystanders in the post office listened closely with averted eyes. At least one decided Dell's hearing must be worsening, judging from how loudly this usually prudent woman was speaking.

Lisa was more than just one of the girls to Dell. A close friendship had grown between the two women. It is hard to be sure whether her husband knew what work she did for Dell, but Lisa's letters from Las Vegas gave an alternate identity there. In May 1977 Lisa wrote that she had been suffering from nephritis but was feeling better, and she complained that Dell had not answered her letters. Hungry for Lusk news, Lisa asked about several local families. In time for Dell's eighty-fifth birthday, Lisa sent a card indicating that her many physical problems were making it hard for her to write. Her health was declining.

It became harder for Dell to maintain the hotel alone. She needed help with housekeeping, and she was lonely. Once she asked Amy Andrews to come to work for her, to keep house, cook, and so on. Although flattered by the offer, Amy was busy tending to her own family. She had enjoyed talking with Dell as she sewed for the girls, but her family needed her. Although Dell reached out into the community a number of times for help, she was apparently unable to find anyone willing to live with her or provide daily services.

At almost three o'clock one crisp fall morning in the mid 1970s, lightly frosted leaves crunched underfoot as a man made his way to the back door of the hotel. He knocked on the door for the longest time and kept hollering, "Need a drink, Dell. Come gimme one."

Dell could see as she peered out a window that the man was dressed only in his shorts. She called the police. "Come get this guy. He's drunk."

After they put the man in the police car and took him away, she asked, "What happened? How come he's undressed?"

"As I understand it, Dell," the policeman said, stifling a grin, "he went on a bender two weeks ago when he got off work."

"He's been drunk that long? How'd he get here?"

"The guys put him in one of the little cabins they have up there with two six packs of beer, figuring he'd taper off. They took all his clothing away, except his shorts, thinking he wouldn't try to leave the room naked."

"So what'll happen to him now?"

"Probably the usual. Either Doc Rust'll dry him out here, or they'll take him to Hot Springs."

Dell nodded. She remembered trips there with Jerry.

Shortly before Thanksgiving Dell was grocery shopping when she noticed an old man who stood shuffling his feet before the array of meat in the meat counter. Dell watched awhile before approaching a salesman and asking him, "What's he doing?"

The salesman told Dell, "I don't know. Maybe it's his way to pass time away. He does it almost every day."

Dell didn't think the man was just passing time. She told the salesman, "I'll tell you what. After I get out of here, you find a nice plump turkey and take it to him. I'll pay for it." They both knew the old man had little money, and she had perceived that he would dearly love to have a piece of meat.

At the same time, Dell would not tolerate shoplifting. One day, as she was buying meat, she noticed the lady in front of her had picked up three packages. At the checkout stand, the lady paid for only one package of meat. Dell was sure the other two packages were inside the lady's coat. On a tip from Dell, the store manager stopped the lady and retrieved the stolen meat.

Lawrence Crofutt sold fuel and repaired furnaces for the C & H Refinery at the west side of Lusk, where Dell bought much of her fuel over the years. One day, she called Lawrence and asked him to work on the hotel's malfunctioning furnace. A while later when Lawrence knocked at the back door, a girl met him there with a knowing wink and invited him upstairs. Dell walked up behind her and said sharply, "Shut up and leave him alone. He's here for the furnace!"

Lawrence's son worked at the refinery after he finished his stint in the Navy, and one day his father told him that Dell needed fuel. "Get her the usual number of gallons and take it out to her."

When Lawrence's son arrived at the hotel, Dell stepped out the back door wearing her coat and said, "You know you've got to take me out to the country place and put fuel in out there?"

"No ma'am, I didn't, but I can handle that," he answered.

She stopped short. "Don't call me ma'am. My name is Dell."

On the drive out, he had to smile about this petite older lady sitting beside him. He remembered the last time he had talked with her. Home on leave from the service, he had decided to see what was happening at the hotel. She had stopped him at the door. "I know both your folks. You're not coming in here."

From time to time, Dell reached out for friendship. While Eddie Plumb had tended bar at the Oasis for Jerry, he and his wife had become friends. The loneliness Dell felt was apparent to Opal when they talked on the telephone. They visited about the ordinary everyday things that were going on; they reminisced about old times. One day, Dell said, "Come down. I've got something to tell you."

Opal had never been inside the hotel and felt somewhat uncomfortable going there. "I'll be there in about thirty minutes."

"Be sure to come to the back door."

When Opal arrived, Dell led the way into her private living room. As they talked, it became obvious Dell didn't have anything in particular to tell her. She wanted to visit.

"Gets lonesome, doesn't it?" Opal, who also lived alone, asked.

"Sure does."

"I like the way you have this arranged." She glanced around the apartment. "The colors are very attractive, and it looks gorgeous."

Afterward, Dell invited her down from time to time to visit.

By the end of hunting season in 1978, Dell more than likely knew she would be out of business soon. One day the town siren went off shortly before noon, assembling volunteers at the fire station for an in-town fire. The number of siren blasts told the approximate location of the fire— a small blaze raged behind the Yellow Hotel. The men set to, and before long they brought it under control. Dell asked them to wait while a table was set up in the backyard. The girls brought out food. Sodas—no alcohol—were provided. The girls who helped serve the meal were attractively dressed and modestly behaved. "Help your-selves," Dell told the men, who picked up plates and gladly moved down the table filling them up. "I wanted to do something special for you men. You do so much for me and the rest of Lusk," Dell told them.

A voucher for $50 dated March 26, 1979, from the Wyoming State Department indicates Dell had paid in full for an outdoor advertis-ing sign. The voucher indicates this was in accordance with the agree-ment Landowner Form R/3024S, dated October 23, 1978. Advertising her business had always required extra ingenuity for Dell.

An abscessed tooth and other physical ailments interfered with Lisa's visit that year. In her Easter card, she wrote: "I hope this finds you in good health. Not too lonely." She asked after several Lusk friends and noted that gas prices were above $1 per gallon. She bemoaned the fact that inflation was terrible and reminded Dell to address letters she sent to her Las Vegas identity—not to Lisa.

One day Dell would never forget was July 4, 1979. She asked the ambulance driver, "How could I trip over some little thing and break my hip? This just doesn't make sense." She had walked along that street for sixty years.

"Nobody likes to break a bone," the orderly assured her gently. "Lie still. We'll be at the hospital shortly." About ten days later Dell was moved to the hospital in Scottsbluff, Nebraska, where she spent nearly two weeks before returning to the Niobrara County Memorial Hospital in Lusk.

In the meantime her Michigan family was planning a trip west. When her great-niece Loraine could not reach Dell, she called the Lusk police department. "I'm sorry, Miss," said the policeman on duty. "Dell Burke is in the hospital in Scottsbluff." By the time the family arrived, Dell had come back to the Lusk Memorial Hospital. Once her health stabilized, she was moved into the nursing home wing. She was never able to return to the Yellow Hotel or her country home.

Finding the right nursing home roommate for Dell turned out to be a challenge. The first one was so horrified by her roommate's identity she called her family to take her out of the home. A more tolerant roommate was soon located.

Dell's family was surprised to discover that even though they had visited in Lusk a number of times only a few people knew about them. Dell had successfully maintained two separate lives. Now, it was time for the family to break through the private walls of Marie Fisher Law, doing business as Dell Burke. Family members talked with the doctor, the banker, the lawyer, and the accountant in Cheyenne, and they learned what Dell's profession had been.

Upon their return home, it was Loraine's task to tell her aunts about Dell Burke. There had always been a mystery about how she was able to make a living in Lusk, but it had never been openly questioned.

Family reactions varied from complete denial to confirmed suspicions. A Nebraska friend had read the 1973 Hillinger article reprinted in her local paper, but she never mentioned it until after Dell died. Because of the distance between Wyoming and Michigan, most family members had never gone west. The extended family maintained only infrequent contact with one another.

Well-wishers from across the country, as well as Luskites, sent get-well cards when they learned Dell was hospitalized. As she felt better, Dell became more mobile and she grew restless. Like most older people who have led an active life, she did not like being confined by hospital walls and she began to plot her departure. Dell remarked to one lady who came by the nursing home to see another resident, "You know, I could be out of this nursing home if I had somebody to look after me."

The lady was dubious. "Oh, yeah?"

"Well, yes," Dell said. "I have a place. All I need is someone to stay with me."

"I don't know whether you could go back."

"Yes," she said. "I could if you helped me a little."

"I have my own home and my own family to take care of, I can't just leave them."

Dell was not to be put off. "I need you. You could come do it."

The lady had seriously mixed feelings and said to herself, "I sort of know what happens to people who stay with her, and I don't want to be part of it."

Next, Dell went to the nursing staff for help. They contacted one of her neighbors. "Think you could take care of Dell?" the staff asked. "She would be at the hotel." Since she had children in high school, the neighbor declined, even though hospital personnel assured her, "You'd get paid better than you were ever paid anywhere else." The neighbor regretted the decision, but knew it was right for her at the time. Dell approached other local women to help take care of her, but she could not find anyone who could or would help her.

As Dell's hip healed, mobility was restored through monitored physical therapy. Nurses and aides helped her walk along the halls to exercise her muscles. Anita Geike was walking with Dell when an attractive young aide zoomed by them.

"She's a lot like one of my girls. She'd sure make a good one," Dell said admiringly, and the aides chuckled. However, their smiles turned to chagrin with Dell's inspection of a heavyset aide. Dell shook her head and said, "Not that one." It became evident that like many older people with illness, injury, or age besetting them in a structured environment, Dell was sometimes confused and thought she was still at home.

After his mother entered the nursing home with Alzheimer's, Butch Bonner visited her there. Seeing Dell in a nearby room one day, Butch stopped by to visit his old neighbor. She seemed to enjoy talking with him and may have remembered him from earlier years.

"Butch, would you do me a favor?" she asked.

"Sure. What is it?"

"Would you go down to the hotel and get my Packard out from underneath and bring it over here?"

"I could do that," he said to keep her from getting agitated. He was sure the Packard was safely parked in the old garage beside the hotel.

"You know something, Butch? I used to run bootleg whiskey from Casper to Lusk in that old Packard."

He settled back to enjoy a round of tales about the old times. The conversation wandered from subject to subject, but Butch suspected what she really wanted was her car so she could go home.

Another visitor had other things on her mind. When she arrived, the TV was turned up loud so Dell could hear it. Since Dell wanted to visit, she asked the lady to turn off the TV. When neither woman could figure out how to turn it off, Dell finally said, "Just pull the plug."

They began visiting and the woman asked, "Dell, did you ever go to church?"

"I was raised in a convent 'til I was twelve."

"Would you like me to come pray with you?"

Dell ignored her and went on talking about other matters.

After a bit the lady said, "I'm not trying to push you, but if you'd like me to come over from time to time and read the Bible with you or pray with you, I'd be glad to."

Dell replied, "Plug the TV in."

The Niobrara County Nursing Home was Dell Burke's last home. She became increasingly forgetful and the vigorous young nurse's aides reminded her of the girls who had worked for her at the hotel.

Even though the nursing staff was there to take care of Dell, she looked for ways to help them. After so many years of taking care of her girls, it was natural that her concern flowed out to the girls around her. When a young aide walked into Dell's room one day with a worried look, Dell became concerned. "Are you okay?" she asked. "Do you have enough to eat?" Dell knew where she had money stashed and could easily pull it out. She kept track of the aides and nurses to make sure they had whatever they needed. She was still "taking care of her girls." The aides were never sure whether Dell's concern for the girls was simply a sincere awareness of needs they might have or if she thought she was still at the hotel taking care of the girls who worked for her.

An older nurse came by her room one day and asked casually,

"Dell, weren't you in the Klondike? How was it up there?"

Dell was puzzled and replied, "I don't know why you'd want to know. You're too old to go into the business now."

Another nurse looked more promising to Dell. As she watched Selma Rogina changing sheets one day, she suddenly said, "Say, you've got a pretty darn good set of legs there." She stood up, swatted Selma on her backside, and offered, "Honey, if you ever want a job, just say the word, and I'll put you to work."

Visitors to the nursing home weren't exempt from her observations either. A lady was on her way to see a friend when Dell walked up to her in the hall and asked hopefully, "Didn't you used to work for me?"

When she needed assistance, Dell thumped a spoon on the bedside table instead of ringing the bell. The staff could not get her to use the bell, nor could they get the spoon away from her. Like most people in her position and her age, there were times she was quite coherent and aware. Sometimes she was not.

Bob Vollmer had already visited his dad down the hall before stepping into Dell's room one evening. Dell looked up at him and hollered, "Dang, Bob, you ain't coming in here. People will talk."

Bob laughed. "Goddamn, we've been good friends all my life, Dell. I don't give a damn what people say." That's how it was with him and his brothers. They had all known her as a friend, not as a madam.

It had been six years since her former accountant Bruce Bergstrom had last seen Dell, but when he heard she had broken a hip, he decided to visit her. At the front desk, he asked, "Is Dell Burke here?"

"Yes, she is."

"Is she taking visitors?"

The nurse nodded and pointed out the common room, where

residents were seated around a table. At first Bruce did not recognize Dell. Her hair was gray, no longer the well-kept auburn. He sat down beside her and quietly asked her, "Dell, remember me?"

She looked at him, but her eyes held no recognition. Although he prompted her with events the two of them would recall, there was no indication she remembered him.

Suddenly she leaned forward, slapped her hand down on the table, and asked, "When is bingo?" Sadly, Bruce realized there was no connection at all.

In mid-October of 1980 Loraine and Phyllis visited Dell once more. It was a good visit with many shared moments and memories. It would be their last one. On the afternoon of November 4, Loraine talked with Dell on the phone. Later that evening, hospital personnel called Loraine to give her the news that her great-aunt had passed away.

The November 11, 1980, edition of *The Lusk Herald* carried a few meager lines about Dell after she died. Even then, her name was misspelled. Her obituary read: "Del (sic) Burke, 93, long-time resident, died at the Niobrara County Nursing Home, Nov. 4. The remains have been cremated. *The Herald* is in the process of contacting a relative of Mrs. Burke for an obituary, but as of this Wednesday morning, contact has not been made."

No further obituary information was printed in *The Lusk Herald*. The funeral record of Marie Fisher Law, aka Dell Burke, noted that she died at the age of ninety-three years, four months, and one day, late in the evening on November 4, from congestive heart failure and pneumonia, tended by Dr. Ken Turner; and that cremation had been ordered. Her occupation was given as "madam (hotel)."

Under the headline "Dell Was a Madam Who Was A Lady," her

longtime friend Red Fenwick wrote in his *Denver Post* column that one of the wealthiest and most charitable women in Wyoming had died virtually unnoticed although the hotel still had a listed telephone number that no one answered. Describing Dell as a "living legend," Fenwick noted that her reputation had crossed state boundaries. His story was picked up by United Press International (UPI).

A couple of months later, under the headline "Lusk 'Madam' Left a $1 Million Estate," Fenwick noted that E. O. Davis, a Cheyenne CPA who had kept Dell's books for many years, had been named executor for Dell's estate, which was estimated to be worth around $1 million. He added that the CPA would be assisted locally by Attorney Bob Pfister to represent Dell's estate interests.

Dell died as quietly as she had lived. She had not been well for some time, and members of the Congregational Church and several other churches in Lusk were praying for her to find peace when she died in her sleep on November 4, 1980. Her girls were gone, some working in other locations and some preceding her in death. The hotel had been closed, and the country place lay in disarray. Word spread quickly among the caring townspeople that this lady had passed on.

THE ESTATE SALE, 1981

Accountant E. O. Davis had his hands full producing a final accounting of Dell's assets, tending to her ashes, meeting with the family, and taking care of details. When he arrived at the bank, he set the cardboard container on the counter. It was in the teller's way, and as she moved it over, she asked, "Now, who left that?"

Another teller, Geneva Burke, pointed at the accountant. As the first teller flipped the box over, Geneva objected. "Those are Dell's ashes."

"Oh, no!" The teller jumped back and wouldn't touch the box again.

Dell's estate included the hotel with eleven lots on First Street in Lusk and the country place house with approximately 495 acres. While Dell had invested heavily in oil, mining, liquor producers, and other companies, some had produced and others had not.

She left four diamond rings, an opal ring, a Gruen watch, and a brown mink coat. Both houses were filled with furniture and personal effects. The final value of the estate was not disclosed, but her four nieces stood to share approximately $500,000 after taxes and final expenses were paid.

Before the estate sale the town of Lusk approached Dell's heirs about purchasing acreage for the town's sewage disposal project.

Amicable negotiations resulted in a transfer of eighty acres to the town.

Several people were interested in purchasing Dell's properties. Across the state, one investor demanded the hotel be turned over to him so it could be reopened as a brothel. None of these deals came to fruition.

Like others spurred by the survival economics of the Depression and World War II, Dell saved many things. "You never know when you'll need it" must have run through her mind as she packed away grocery bags, newspapers, string, wire, and boxes of empty mayonnaise jars.

Her black book, containing income records and potentially compromising information, was handed over to the lawyers. Contrary to local opinion that Dell took in only cash, records show she accepted an occasional check from customers, including one who indicated his check was for "labor."

Disposition of the estate was turned over to Madden Brothers Auction Company. Items from the country house were matched with ones at the hotel to form sets. Unopened boxes of sheets, clothing, and supplies sat on hotel beds. Boxes of toys Dell had purchased for the children of her girls, along with letters from girls recalling her kindnesses, were discovered. The set of sterling that was monogrammed with the letter "L" (Law) was located behind the bathtub along with the vanity set monogrammed with the letter "M" (Mahaffey). These became the property of Dell's heirs.

The press release sent to United Press International (UPI) described the highlights of Dell's career. The Associated Press (AP) picked up the story, and the estate sale on August 14 and August 15, 1981, hit newspapers from New York to California, from Montana to Texas, and overseas in the *Pacific Stars and Stripes.*

Lusk's population of 1,650 increased to more than 3,000 that weekend. Hotel and motel rooms, as well as public campgrounds, were filled for miles around. Restaurants and stores accustomed to closing early stayed open late each night. On Friday afternoon enthusiastic crowds gathered at Dell's country place to view and buy dishes, furniture, linens, Christmas decorations, and lawn equipment. Auctioneer Lex Madden hopped on top of the chicken coop to go through his paces.

Seated under the birch and pine trees Jerry had planted, treasure hunters sought respite from the heat. A large balding man leaned over to his neighbor and began a conversation. "Did you hear about the guy who called the Yellow Hotel one evening and asked for Dell?"

"What'd they say?"

"'She's outta town.' Then the guy asks, 'Where's she at?'"

"And?"

"'At the best damn whorehouse in England.'" He chuckled and continued. "You know, she didn't like lawyers, clergy, or politicians. Like, when she needed some legal work done she might go to Attorney Stan Hathaway. Then for some fool reason, she'd get pissed off with him, and go see Attorney Jim Barrett."

"Guess she got over it some. I heard she kept on working with ol' Barrett even after he was elected governor."

"She always said she had friends in high places."

That evening, a crowd of two thousand toured the Yellow Hotel. Navajo rugs, clothing, pictures, and paintings were displayed in the reception room. Traffic was routed through the front door, along the hallway past the reception room and up the stairs into the working rooms. As they passed pictures displayed along the walls, one family stopped to gape at a picture that matched one in their family's barn, sparking conjecture that a bachelor uncle might have given that to Dell.

Stories abounded during the tour and sale. One man who was walking down the stairs ahead of his wife commented, "That step always did squeak." His wife's reaction was not reported.

Auction fever was rampant the next day during the sale. Tourists from as far away as Florida wandered the streets in anticipation. Preparing to hold auctions simultaneously on two sides of the hotel, auctioneers Lex and Shawn Madden dressed in ruffled tuxedo shirts with black garters on their sleeves, velvet bow ties around their necks, and black silk hats topped their heads. "Where else can you get a madam's dressing gown or her silk stockings?" they taunted the crowd. Shawn took bids on furniture, kitchen appliances, and utensils at the side of the hotel, while Lex sold clothes, shoes, purses, and hats at the front.

The well-traveled path from the nearby train station to the Yellow Hotel's dimly lit back door was still visible. Local entrepreneurs hawked yellow buttons with turtledoves in a compromising position under the words "Dell's Hotel—60 years of Lust in Lusk" and yellow T-shirts that said, "I got a piece of the old west at Dell's Yellow Hotel, Lusk, Wyoming."

A group was gathered around the stand serving "Sloppy Joe hot-dogs." After a while, a rancher commented, "You couldn't get away with anything around ol' Dell."

"Oh really?" a woman exclaimed.

"Yeah," he went on, "one time, this ol' boy got himself in a bad way with his missus, and told Dell all about it. Dell had him sit a little spell, and then sent him upstairs. When he got inside the bedroom door, he almost came right back out."

"How come?"

"Well, there stood his missus, with a smile on her face."

"Uh oh! She work there or Dell set him up?"

"He never said, and he didn't tell the divorce judge about it, either."

A businessman had been listening to the conversation. He turned to the rancher. "Ever hear about the time the judge got drunk and fell down in the alley? It was a really cold winter night, and he was wearing his usual fur coat and beaver hat."

"I heard about that. Happened in the early days of Lusk, didn't it?"

"Yeah. Well, along come the highway patrolman and another man. They took off the judge's coat and hat and the patrolman put them on. The two went over to Dell's, where they took pictures of the patrolman shaking hands with Dell. Of course, his face didn't show."

"The judge never knew for sure if they'd played a trick on him."

The sun began to sink, and many drifted away to consider their purchases over dinner or a drink. The auction moved inside when a rainstorm came up, and the sale of smaller items continued until nearly 10:00 p.m. Throughout the day reporters from the ABC, NBC, and CBS television networks had used cameras and recording equipment to pick up priceless stories, and newspaper reporters worked the crowd for quotes about Dell.

Laughter and music could be heard blocks away. Cars filled First Street and jammed adjacent streets beyond capacity.

Auctioneers Lex and Shawn, along with co-worker Cody Thompson, wisecracked their way through racy items, including pillows "which might have many stories to tell," douche pans, silk stockings, bras, billfolds and belongings left behind by customers, and one hundred boxes of Dell's size 6AA shoes. Room keys, the clock that had signaled the end of a session, rainbow-colored silk stockings, silver whistles, and an oriental dressing gown with silk and gold thread were hot sellers. The 1932 Mills Studio jukebox and a Wurlitzer juke box, both fully functional, were strongly contested items. The 1955 Chrysler New Yorker Deluxe went to Merle Hahn, Gamble's Hardware Store manager.

Nursing home staff and neighbors swore Dell had always had her own teeth, but a set of false teeth reputed to be Dell's sold for $15. Furniture, furs, jewelry, dishes, flatware, prints, paintings—fine expensive items as well as everyday "junk"—went for surprising prices. Probably the biggest surprise was the difficulty in selling the old iron single beds, most of which brought only $4 to $5 each.

Other sale items included leather benches used by gentlemen waiting their turn ($17 on Friday, $120 and $400 on Saturday), dog blankets marked Yen Chee and Chi Chi ($8 each), Navajo rugs (large $1,550, small $191), a coal-and-wood-burning stove ($250), a modern electric stove ($1), Roseville pottery ($110), an antique lamp with hanging beads ($495), Fiesta Ware dishes ($420), and two bedroom suites ($1,100 and $355). Nearly 1,300 items were listed on eighty-six buyer sheets.

Buyers from New Mexico, Florida, California, Idaho, Colorado, Montana, North and South Dakota, Nebraska, and other western states joined bidders from all across Wyoming. Local antiques collectors with basements full of their own Western memorabilia took home items from the hotel. The Singer sewing machine found a home with Amy Andrews, who had provided seamstress services to Dell and her girls. A Maytag washer went to the Cook family. Ed and Wilma Baldwin picked up a room key for their collection. Mary Engebretson purchased stockings and clothing that she sometimes displays. The Charlie Russell prints became the prized possessions of Sheriff Bebe Reed, and the glass-topped table made by a sheepherder was among Joe Andrews's purchases.

Two of Dell's great-nieces, Loraine Fisher and Norma Vecellio, attended the sale. During the hotel tour Friday, Loraine was presented with a watch originally worn by Dell's mother. Loraine told one news reporter that her great aunt was a fine business woman, who was generous but also knew how to make good money. She admitted that until two years earlier she had been unaware that her great-aunt was really one of the last notorious madams of the Rocky Mountain West. Nonetheless, Loraine was very proud of Dell and knew her to be a fine person who would have enjoyed the atmosphere of the sale, had she been there. During the weekend, the nieces scattered Dell's ashes at the country place.

When the sale was over, two local men were the owners of Dell's real estate. Joe Madden (father of the auctioneers) had acquired the hotel for $41,500, and Charles Christian had purchased the country place and lands for $173,000. Christian planned to incorporate the newly acquired property, which completely adjoined his land on the east side, into the total operation of Christian Stables.

Across the country, memorabilia from the sale was placed in homes from California, to New York, Florida, and Texas. Items ranged from the hotly pursued old jukeboxes to sterling earrings with prices that ranged from expected highs to unexpected lows. Some people purchased items for memories, some for investment to sell later, and some just because they wanted "a piece of the Old West" from the Yellow Hotel as proclaimed on a T-shirt sold by young entrepreneurs the day of the sale.

There is no doubt that Dell's estate sale will stand out in the memories of those who attended, as well as some who would have loved to attend but distance kept them away. The memorabilia still provides a silent reminder of the old days at the Yellow Hotel and its unique little auburn-haired owner.

THE DEMISE OF THE YELLOW HOTEL, 2007

The sale of the Yellow Hotel and its adjoining lots was considered in two ways. In one the hotel and lots were auctioned off as a unit. In the second the hotel and the adjoining lots were bid on as separate entities. The seller could choose between them.

Joe Andrews's bid appeared to be last and highest when bidding on the hotel was stopped for consultation with the family. While they discussed it, Joe made bank arrangements to pay for the hotel that he planned to turn into a supper club/museum. When he returned, he learned that Dell's family had accepted a different bid, which included the lots and the hotel.

Joe Madden purchased the property located at 208 Griffith Boulevard (formerly West First Street), Lusk OT (Original Town), Block 4, Lots 2-12, for $41,500. Reportedly, he planned to convert it into a rooming house on the upper floor and a restaurant on the ground floor. Sometime during 1982 Joe leased the building to house railroad workers, and during this use the building sustained considerable damage.

The following year Madden revealed plans to remodel the interior and provide mobile home parking spaces on the grounds. The Lusk Town Council granted permission for him to use what was originally plotted as an alley along with a small "pie-shaped" piece of property adjacent to his. Apparently the Wyoming Historical Society had requested that the exterior of the hotel building be kept in its original state. In 1985 Madden put the hotel property along with twenty-three nearby lots up for sale. By then he believed the real estate's value had increased due to the added real property and the furniture and refurbishing that had been done, and he estimated the property to be worth $16,000. Joe Madden's intentions seem to have been aimed at making it an economic investment, but apparently he did not succeed.

At one point the hotel came under the jurisdiction of his former wife, who considered placing an ad in the *Wall Street Journal* that would read "Elderly Wyoming Christian woman, who through legal flukes, ended up with bordello. Name best price." When she discovered the ad would cost $750, she signed the property over to Madden's estate.

In the mid-1990s, a Lusk middle-school class wanted to help renovate the hotel, but the mayor told them the building was beyond restoration.

Dell had always maintained the buildings and grounds with regular paint jobs and lawn work. When it was sold in 1981, the hotel could have been converted into a frontier museum, capitalizing on the bordello aspect. Converting it into a steak house, supper club, bed-and-breakfast, or rooming house were other options. The honky-tonk atmosphere could have been revived. Dell's family members chose not to establish a historic establishment or run a commercial enterprise so distant from their residences. And no one stepped forward before the sale with these aspirations.

A few Luskites might have preferred that the old hotel be torn down. They strongly disfavored promoting "that kind of institution" in Lusk, as it is seen as approving of prostitution. Others see the demise of the hotel as the end of an era, in addition to the end of a building, which could have been preserved and provided tourist income.

After Madden's death, the hotel became part of his estate and proceedings pended for some years. Over the years, visitors have removed doors, doorknobs, and other pieces of the hotel. Vandals have spray painted walls and shattered windows. Water pipes have frozen and broken, which has caused serious deterioration of the flooring on both levels. On May 15, 2007, the dilapidated properties were sold at auction. Two businessmen who graduated from Lusk High School in the 1950s purchased the hotel buildings. Plans are under way to renovate the buildings into a bed and breakfast with restaurant and gift shop, honoring Dell Burke's persona and era.

As the last functioning brothel of its kind in the region and one that spanned the years from pioneer to modern times, the Yellow Hotel holds a special place in the history of frontier towns of the West.

EPILOGUE

A legend is a story handed down through generations and popularly believed to have a historical basis though it may not be verifiable. Because legends are passed down orally, details may be added to explain the unknown, and over the years some of these details may change.

Marie Fisher Law, dba Dell Burke, did not share her private life. Most people in Lusk knew little about her family, and her family knew little about her professional life.

The following anecdotes undoubtedly contain some fiction, yet these stories are included in a book of nonfiction because they were repeated often enough by people who knew her to merit inclusion.

Why Prostitution?

No one really knows what caused Marie Fisher to turn to prostitution. The fact remains that she married at age seventeen, and when she separated from Stephen J. Law about seven years later, she was still beautiful, no longer virgin, but capable and intelligent. She had few job skills to support herself.

Circumstantial evidence suggests that Dell may have discovered her husband had been married to another woman the entire time they were together. Records concerning the end of her marriage could not be located.

Whatever propelled Marie into prostitution, it was significant enough to cause her to make the tremendous leap from her traditional Lutheran upbringing. Based on her extreme discretion about her profession, it is probable she dealt with deep shame.

Marie Fisher Law took her circumstances, her abilities, and her appearance and made the most of them. She was successful. She conducted herself discreetly with the ethics and conduct befitting a well-mannered lady. She invested in people, the town of Lusk, and the western region, as well as in businesses, companies, and corporations.

Why Lusk?

Dell may have been approached by Casper bootleggers to help handle their whiskey trade in the Lusk–Lance Creek area in exchange for legal protection. She told friends that she had been over the back roads in South Dakota, making deliveries, and her car was rumored to contain a hidden compartment in the floor, where she carried moonshine.

She told Charles Hillinger in 1973 that she thought the name of the town was Lust, which made it an appropriate next stop.

Still another story is that she had two sisters in the area. However, family records show that Dell was the only daughter of Almeda and John Fisher, and she had only three older brothers. None of the brothers or their wives made Lusk their home.

She Must Have Been Highly Educated and Widely Traveled

Dell was an excellent conversationalist. She could talk with anybody about almost anything. She asked sensible questions and had a well-developed sense of humor. Her conversational ability suggested a good education. She was also a skilled raconteur who produced a compelling story. She read widely and used the information in her stories.

Her handwriting was attractive and easy to read. She wrote appropriate notes of appreciation, congratulations to acquaintances, and other letters to her family and friends.

In 1969 Dell told her accountant she had attended a Catholic academy in Grand Forks, North Dakota. However, no family history supports this. The family was strongly Lutheran and was making a meager living in the rough frontier of North Dakota. Dell was the youngest of four children, and none of her three brothers received higher education.

Family records indicate that she attended school in Ohio through the fourth grade and continued her education in a back room of the family's North Dakota store. Dell's claim of receiving a Catholic education was not supported by family information.

Records show that Dell regularly purchased many magazines, including *Esquire, Bazaar, In Wyoming, Time, Ladies Home Journal, Vogue, National Geographic, Exchange,* and the *Wyoming Pictorial Magazine.* She also subscribed to many newspapers, including the *Scottsbluff Daily Herald, Wyoming State Tribune,* the *Farm Journal, The Lusk Herald,* and *Colorado Rancher and Farmer,* as well as *Dunn's Review,* and *Status and Diplomat.* She was also known to read many books and especially enjoyed historical novels.

She told several acquaintances that from the age of sixteen to eighteen she was married to a man in Malta, Montana, but his family did not accept her and "ran her off." Although her mother's scrapbook contains a newspaper clipping about a marriage planned when she was sixteen, family records show that only one marriage was consummated, and that was to Canadian Stephen Law the following year.

Dell enjoyed traveling. Records and photographs indicate that she spent time in Canada, Alaska, Mexico, and Hawaii and that she traveled extensively through Arizona, Texas, and California. Claims of her travel to the Orient could not be validated.

Friends

Dell was considered a charming, caring woman. Except for the offensive fence she erected between her property and the Smiths on First Street, Dell was considered a good neighbor.

Jerry Dull played an important part in Dell's life for many years, yet publicly they maintained a casual relationship. Few people knew about the trips they took to California or realized they lived together at the country place part of the time. Exactly when they got together is unclear, but it is likely the attraction solidified while she took care of him after he lost his foot in the 1930 oil-field accident.

Dell had other friends. Her business partnership with Jerry and Maynard Bishop led to social interaction with Maynard's wife and daughter. She spent time with the Plumbs; Eddie tended bar at the Oasis. Dell visited with Hester and Bill Smith Sr. and members of the Vollmer family. Among her other friends were the Duff Hollon family, the Bergstroms, Jim Griffith, and Don Whiteaker. Several friendly episodes were reported with other women. Although there is little record, it is likely that she continued her friendships with some of the people who left Lusk for Cheyenne and other places.

She Must Have Been Rich

Dell Burke was widely considered an astute businesswoman who knew how to make money and how to invest it. She claimed that she made

$10,000 one year in the pre-Depression days in Alaska. Other stories indicate her income in Montana was as much as $100,000.

Everyone said she had to be rich. Otherwise how could she contribute to charitable organizations, educate kids, travel, loan the city of Lusk nearly $15,000 in 1929, run a hotel, and own a country place.

A counter belief is that Jerry Dull was the one with money. That coming out of his oil-field work, he had money, and his funds were used to buy the country place. Further, his gambling and bootlegging brought in a good income. It was rumored that Dell distributed his whiskey, and in the 1950s he set Dell up in business. Actually, the hotel had been in business about thirty years by then.

Other stories indicate that when Jerry hurt his leg in the oil-field accident, he was nearly destitute, and that Dell took him in. The country place was purchased after he was injured but before he had a chance to recoup with bar income. After her death, newspapers across the nation asserted she left behind between $275,000 and $1 million.

Did Dell Have Power?

There is no doubt Dell had power in Lusk, as well as across the region. She operated an illegal business with little legal intervention from 1919 until 1987. It was a commonly held belief that Dell loaned the city of Lusk money for the water and electric plant and possibly for the sewer system.

One resident of Lusk remembers hearing Dell admit she loaned the town the money to keep the power plant going, and that's why they didn't try to stop her business. Another informant remembers Dell commenting that she owned 51 percent of the light plant and saying, "It'll be the darkest town in the state of Wyoming if they close me down."

Still other residents remember hearing Dell deny she ever said that. She may have told different people different stories at different times. Oral historians note this frequently occurs.

According to numerous sources, Dell bailed out the town of Lusk by buying most of the bonds required for the purchase of new power plant equipment in 1930. It is likely they were call bonds, and Dell could have called them in any time before they were due. This is not the same as "closing Lusk down" or "cutting off their lights," but it would have placed the city in a serious financial bind.

Another myth surrounding Dell is related to her political connections. She is reputed to have known and entertained a number of high Wyoming state officials. It is possible she made generous but discreet contributions to the political objectives of influential people who in turn made it possible for her to continue in business. At least one governor reportedly provided her with legal services.

An interesting but repudiated story describes a time when a postal worker believed Dell's hotel should be closed. Dell is said to have retaliated by having the sheriff padlock the post office doors because Dell owned the building. However, that building belonged to Paul Godfrey, not to Dell Burke.

Dell contributed generously to most or all of the local churches, one of which gained windows thanks to her beneficence. Other congregations received support for their building funds. It is likely this made it harder for the church people to make serious efforts to oust her.

She Put a Number of Kids through College

Reports about Dell funding young adults' college educations were made so frequently it seems impossible to believe they were all just rumors.

Although these reports could not be validated, they add to her legend. Dell told people she helped kids go to college, but she never divulged the recipients' names. She was quoted by Charles Hillinger as saying she had "sent two boys through college, one Stanford, the other UCLA. They both got Ph.D.s." She commented recipients did not know she helped them because it was done through scholarships.

One mother told a neighbor that Dell had financed her sons' education, but other family members vehemently denied this connection. Another possible recipient apparently bragged to a friend about receiving Dell's support, but again, other family members denied it.

While it was impossible to prove whom Dell helped educate, it is believed she helped at least a dozen families. Although their identities could not be conclusively established, a profile of recipients could be drawn. Each was a bright, intelligent, and physically active boy. Interests varied but all the boys clearly benefited from higher education. A small number were already troublemakers, and others had that potential. They have all gone on to professional standings in Wyoming and across the nation, and many still hold a strong allegiance to Dell.

Why so much discretion? Dell may have believed her line of work could jeopardize the future standing of recipients if her connection were known. Some people may have chosen not to disclose this because they were embarrassed to admit where assistance came from or that they needed financial help at all. Another theory is that fathers of recipients may have spent money at the Yellow Hotel and wished to be unknown for obvious reasons.

Tributes to a Legend

Lusk is probably remembered by more people for the Yellow Hotel than for any other single person, event, or place. Whether it be from notoriety, fame, or infamy, the hotel brought attention and publicity to Lusk, and Dell Burke was in business longer than almost any other business of Lusk.

Dell is part of the history of Lusk, of Niobrara County, of Wyoming, and of the western frontier. Note was taken of her contributions in a Niobrara County history by Mae Urbanek in 1984, who wrote: "Another noted character of Niobrara County was Madam Dell Burke of Lusk. She received statewide publicity for her establishment, and for her generosity in giving great sums of money for civic improvement and charity."

A quilt block, souvenir pins, a child's perception of a Lusk business, a history by Larry K. Brown with reference to ladies who commemorate Dell annually, songs, poetry, and numerous personal collections all serve as reminders of her participation in history as the frontier moved forward.

In the early 2000s, Ross Diercks, Wyoming state representative and Niobrara County High School teacher, wrote lyrics and music for his song, "Bring Back the Yellow Hotel and the Wild Ol' Buckaroo." The following is an excerpt.

> *Madame Dell had the Yellow Hotel and her ladies*
> *looked so fine*
> *Sweet perfume, cozy rooms, and one hot-lovin' time*
> *But she sent 'em to church on Sundays*

Some kids to college, too

And in the days of the Depression

She helped pull the whole town through

(chorus)

Saturday night, dodgin' the fights

Play a little poker if your luck feels right

Slammin' shots of whiskey

Feelin' kinda risky

Better hunt some lovin' before you get too tipsy

We don't need no hoity-toity people tellin' us what to do

Bring back the Yellow Hotel and the wild ol' Buckaroo.

In the late 1980s, Marilyn Kutzli from Andover, Iowa, was inspired to write a poem about the hotel and its business. An excerpt from her poem "The Yellow Hotel" reads:

Come listen to my story

About the yellow hotel in Lusk,

Still standing proud, but shabby

With its faded paint and dust.

The long, true tale was told me

as we rode through that western town.

Dell Burke was noted for her congeniality

With the money that she earned

She started a hotel and bordello.

Whether they liked her or not, or whether they even knew her, Lusk residents could not completely ignore Dell Burke. Like a thread on the loom of small-town life, Dell and the Yellow Hotel are an integral part of the history of the western frontier.

INTERVIEWEES AND CONTRIBUTORS

Akers, Kester, interview, Lusk, Wyoming, July 2004.

Allen, Orval & Diane, interview, Lusk, Wyoming, July 2001.

Andrews, Amy & Joe, interview, Lusk, Wyoming, July 2002.

Baker, Faye & Harry, interview, Lusk, Wyoming, June 2002.

Baldwin, Wilma, interview, Prairie Center, Wyoming, August 2001.

Bales, Velma Jean (Reckling), letter, Laramie, Wyoming, June 2001.

Bardo, Jane, interview, Douglas, Wyoming, August 2002.

Barrett, Jim, telephone, Cheyenne, Wyoming, June 2001.

Bergstrom, Bruce & Barbara, interview, Greybull, Wyoming, July 2001.

Blackmore, Bob, e-mail, Casper, Wyoming, July 2001.

Boner, Polly, interview, Lusk, Wyoming, July 2001, March 2006.

Bonner, Butch, telephone, North Carolina, January 2004.

Bonsell, Beverly (Walker) & Roger, interview, Lusk, Wyoming, June 2001.

Boyer, Dotty (Shoopman), telephone, Bennett, Colorado, July 2002.

Bredthauer, Jackie, interview, Lusk, Wyoming, June 2001.

Brown, Harry, interview, Lusk, Wyoming, July 2001.

Brown, Larry K., e-mail, Cheyenne, Wyoming, spring 2006.

Brummell, Helen, interview, Torrington, Wyoming, June 2001.

Bryant, Howard F. "Burr" & Winifred, interview, Lusk, Wyoming, June 2001.

Burke, Geneva, interview, Lusk, Wyoming, August 2002.

Clarke, Della, interview, Lusk, Wyoming, July 2002.

Cook, Ed, interview, Lusk, Wyoming, August 2002.

Costopolous, Barbara, interview, Guernsey, Wyoming, July 2001.

Crofutt, Dave & Barbara, Lusk, Wyoming, June 2001.

Darrow, Bob, interview, Lakewood, Colorado, June 2002.

Davis, Claire (Smith) & Bill Kennedy, interview, Lusk, Wyoming, July 2002.

Diercks, Ross, interview, Lusk, Wyoming, August 2002.

Fagan, Madelein (Ladwig), interview, Casper, Wyoming, July 2002.

Ferris, Darlene, interview, Lusk, Wyoming, July 2001.

Fisher, Loraine, e-mails (January 2001–May 2006), letters (July 2001, July 2003), interview (May 2004), personal collection, Detroit, Michigan.

Fleming, Ruth, interview, Lusk, Wyoming, August 2002.

Foreman, Mary Anne (Griffith), interview, Lusk, Wyoming, July 2002.

Geike, Anita & Wendell, interview, Lusk, Wyoming, May 2001.

Hahn, Phyllis (Willson) & Merle, interviews and conversations, Lusk, Wyoming, February 2000, August 2000, 2001–2007.

Hahn, Stan, interview, Casper, Wyoming, June 2001.

Hanson, Ernie, interview, Lusk, Wyoming, June 2001.

Harris, Bryan, interview, Torrington, Wyoming, July 2001.

Haynes, Vearl (O'Connor), telephone, Folsom, California, July 2004.

Hollon, Jerry, interview, Laramie, Wyoming, July 2002.

Holm, Flora, interview, Douglas, Wyoming, August 2002.

Hunter, Kathleen, interview, Torrington, Wyoming, August 2002.

Johnson, Betty (Myrup), telephone, Casper, Wyoming, June 2001.

Johnson, Don & Gloria (Vogel), interview, Wheatland, Wyoming, June 2002.

Johnson, Doris, interview, Lusk, Wyoming, June 2001.

Jordan, Dorothy, interview, Lusk, Wyoming, July 2001.

Jugler, Wanda, personal conversation, Lusk, Wyoming, July 2002.

Kee, Leslie, e-mail, Lusk, Wyoming, February 2004.

Kilmer, Mike, interview, Casper, Wyoming, July 2002.

Ladwig, Harold, interview, Douglas, Wyoming, August 2002.

Ladwig, Richard & Mildred (Pinkerton), interview, Manville, Wyoming, August 2002.

Larson, Jim, Jack, & Kathy, interview, Lusk, Wyoming, June 2002.

Larson, Noal, interview, Lusk, Wyoming, August 2001.

Lauer, Arthur "Archie," interview, Lusk, Wyoming, June 2001.

Madden, Glenna, interview, Lusk, Wyoming, June 2001.

Minear, Vickie, e-mail, July 2004.

Moore, Jean (Panno), interview, La Habra, California, July 2002.

Percival, Betty, interview, Lusk, Wyoming, June 2002.

Peterson, Denis, interview, Lusk, Wyoming, July 2002.

Pfister, Robert E., interview, Lusk, Wyoming, August 2002.

Plumb, Opal, interview, Lusk, Wyoming, July 2002.

Price, Suzie, interview, Lusk, Wyoming, June 2001.

Rapp, Eddie, interview, Lusk, Wyoming, August 2002.

Reed, S.C. "Bebe," interview, Lusk, Wyoming, August 2002.

Rising, Lynn, interview, Lusk, Wyoming, July 2001.

Ruffing, Bess (Mrs. Jennings), interview, Lusk, Wyoming, June 2002.

Ruffing, John, interview, Lusk, Wyoming, June 2002.

Smith, Hester, interview, Lusk, Wyoming, June 2002.

Taylor, Ray, interview, Lusk, Wyoming, August 2002.

Titchener, Al & Eva, interview, Lusk, Wyoming, July 2001.

Tollman, Julie, interview, Lusk, Wyoming, July 2002.

Vollmer, Bob, interviews, Lusk, Wyoming, June 2001, August 2002.

Watson, Bud & Virginia, interview, Torrington, Wyoming, July 2002.

Whiteaker, Don, interview, Lusk, Wyoming, August 2002.

Williams, Terry and Dana, personal conversation, Lusk, Wyoming, June 2001.

Willson, Brad, telephone, Issaquah, Washington, December 2003.

Willson, Jim, interview, Lusk, Wyoming, February 2000.

Wilson, Mary Jean (Willson), Chuck & Dan, interview, Sundance, Wyoming, July 2001.

Wood, Katherine E., telephone conversation, Alcova, Wyoming, July 2002.

BIBLIOGRAPHY

Albert, Alexa. *Brothel; Mustang Ranch and Its Women*. New York: Random House, 2001.

Allen, June. *Dolly's House; The story of Ketchikan's last legal Madam and Her Creek Street Home*. Ketchikan, AK: Rainforest Publishing, Dolly's Enterprises, 1991.

Allemand, Roy V. *Blizzard 1949,* n.d.

Allende, Isabel. *Daughter of Fortune*, New York: Harper Perennial, 1999.

Bagne, Mark. "Dell Burke's Brothel Sold Out for $300,000," *Wyoming State Tribune*, Cheyenne, Wyoming, August 17, 1981.

Bartimus, Tad. "Beds best bordello bargains; 3,000 turn out for Lusk auction," *Star-Tribune*, Casper, Wyoming, August 16, 1981.

Baumler, Ellen. "Devil's Perch: Prostitution from Suite to Cellar in Butte, Montana," 1996. unpublished manuscript, Montana History Conference, Butte.

Baggott, Julianna. *The Madam*, New York: Atria Books, 2003.

Billings Gazette, "Bordello treasures bring big dollars," Billings, Montana, August 16, 1981.

Bonner, Larry. *The Big Rawhide Butte*. Cary, NC: ebook, 2003.

Brown, Larry K. "The Lusty Lady of Lusk," *Wyoming Annals 66,* no. 4, Winter 1994-1995.

———. "The Lusty Lady of Lusk: Dell Burke followed the male trail to Wyoming," *Casper Star-Tribune,* August 23, 1998.

Bryant, Winifred (Project Director). *The War Years, a 50th Anniversary Album.* Niobrara Country, Wyoming, n.d.

Butler, Anne M. *Daughters of Joy, Sisters of Misery: Prostitutes in the American West 1865-90.* Urbana & Chicago: University of Illinois Press, 1987.

Chamblin, Thomas (ed.). *The Historical Encyclopedia of Wyoming.* Cheyenne, WY: Wyoming Historical Institute, ca. 1970.

Cheyenne Tribune-Eagle, "Local Songwriter Pens Ode to Dell," Cheyenne, Wyoming, August 16, 1981.

Cicmanec-Pier Funeral Home. "Funeral Record of Marie Fisher Law," Lusk, Wyoming, November 7, 1980.

Citizenship Records, State Historical Society of North Dakota.

City of Lusk Police Docket, 1919–1935.

Compton's Pictured Encyclopedia and Fact-Index, 1947 edition. Chicago: F. E. Compton & Company, 1947.

Davis, John W. *Sadie and Charlie: The Lives and Times of Sadie and Charlie Worland.* Worland, WY: Washakie Publishing Company, 1989.

Dell Burke Collection, Wyoming Pioneer Memorial Museum, Douglas, Wyoming.

Ellis, Sue F. *Dell Burke's Yellow Hotel,* unpublished manuscript, History of the West 121, WY, 1987.

Essman, Ray (ed.). *Only Count the Sunny Hours, Madame Isabelle's Diary*. Winona, MN: Apollo Books, 1981.

Evans, Max. *Madam Millie: Bordellos from Silver City to Ketchikan*, Albuquerque, NM: University of New Mexico Press, 2002.

Fenwick, Red. *Red Fenwick's West: Yesterday and Today*. Denver: Sage Books, 1956.

———. "Dell Was a Madam Who Was a Lady," *The Denver Post*, November 30, 1980.

———. "Dell's Profession No Embarrassment . . . the Madam Was a Well-Heeled Lady," *The Denver Post*, December 21, 1980.

———. "Town Roars Alive in Bawdy Auction—Estate of Madam," *The Denver Post*, August 16, 1981.

———. "Search for Mystery-shrouded 'Queen of the Sandbar' is Ended," *The Denver Post*, August 23, 1981.

Franscell, Ron. "Last Bawdy house trinkets gone, but memories linger," *Star-Tribune*, Casper, Wyoming, August 17, 1981.

"Girls of the Gulch," *Deadwood Magazine*, July/August 1997.

Griffin, Susan. *The Book of the Courtesans: A Catalogue of Their Virtues*. New York: Broadway Books, 2001.

Griffith, Jim. *A Funny Thing Happened on the Way to the Capitol*. 1988.

Hanson, Dan. *Rare Old Fair Old Golden Days*, no date.

Hillinger, Charles. "Everybody Likes Dell—But Most Avoid Her." *Los Angeles Times*, March 26, 1973.

Jones, Walter. *The Sandbar*, Casper, WY: BASO, Inc., 1981.

Kimball, Nell. *Nell Kimball: Her life As An American Madam by Herself*. New York: The Macmillan Company, 1970.

Lawrence, Tom. *Wyoming Whorehouses: A 100 year historical and humorous observation*. Buffalo, WY, n.d.

Lusk Free Lance. Lusk, Wyoming, July 31, 1930.

Lusk Herald. Lusk, Wyoming, Golden Jubilee Edition, 1936; February 27, 1936; April 9, 1936; April 9, 1936.

———. "Heart Attack Claims Jerry Dull at Wheel of Car Saturday Night," June 9, 1955.

———. November 13, 1980. Del [sic] Burke, obituary.

———. "Many Attend Estate Sale," August 20, 1981.

———. "Hotel, ranch and belongings sell for total of $275,000," August 20, 1981.

———. "People, Places Outlined in History," February 9, 1984

Lusk Herald and Van Tassell Pioneer, Lusk, Wyoming: March 27, 1919; January 6, 1920; July 2, 1920; August 27, 1920; February 7, 1928; March 9, 1928; March 15, 1928; March 22, 1928; April 26, 1928; March 7, 1929; April 11, 1929; June 6, 1929; July 12, 1929.

———. "Abatement Suspends Operation," March 6, 1930.

———. May 22, 1930; July 24, 1930; April 18, 1935.

Miller, Ronald Dean. *Shady Ladies of the West*. Los Angeles: Westernlore Press, 1964.

Newsom, Jim. "Former bordello up for sale," *Star-Tribune*, Casper, Wyoming, April 20, 1985.

Niobrara County Court Records, Lusk, Wyoming.

Niobrara County Tax Assessors Records, tax listing for 1920.

Pacific Stars and Stripes (compiled from AP and UPI), "The last hurrah of Wyo. Bordello," August 17, 1981.

Pitcher, Don. *Wyoming Handbook including Yellowstone and Grand Teton National Parks.* Moon Travel Handbooks), 1997.

Reckling, Walter "Doc." unpublished manuscript, 1948, Velma Jean Bales Collection.

Seagraves, Anne. *Soiled Doves: Prostitution in The Early West.* Hayden, ID: Wesannne Publications, 1994.

Stephens, Autumn. *Wild Women: Crusaders, Curmudgeons and Completely Corsetless Ladies in the Otherwise Virtuous Victorian Era.* Berkeley, CA: Conari Press, 1992.

U.S. Census Bureau, U.S. Federal Census, prepared by Wyoming Department of A & I, Division of Economic Analysis, 1910, 1920, 1930, 1940, 1950, 1960, 1970.

Van Nuys Daily News, "Bordello auction nets $300,000 from sale of 'soiled dove' souvenirs," Van Nuys, California, (ca. August 1981).

Whitehead, Anne Willson. *A History of Manville, Wyoming and the Manville Ranching Community.* n.d.

Willson, Helen. "Old Mother Featherlegs, Ike Diapert and George McFadden Share Lonely Grave Along the Trail," *Reminiscences of the Founding and Growth of the Town of Lusk,* ca. 1936.

Wyoming Pioneer Association, *Pages from Converse County* (Wheelock, Ben and Margaret "Maggie"), 1986.

Wyoming Statutes 1957, Vol. 3, by Authority of Chapter 155, Session Laws of 1955 and Chapter 172, Session Laws of 1957, quoting Approval on February 14, 1921.

ABOUT THE AUTHOR

June Willson Read was raised on a cattle ranch a few miles outside of Lusk, Wyoming. She studied journalism at the University of Wyoming, where she met and married Al Read. She received her bachelor's and master's degrees from the University of North Carolina at Greensboro, and later earned a Ph.D. in marriage and family intervention from Texas Tech University. Her psychotherapy career spanned twenty years in Texas, Wyoming, and North Carolina.

She became interested in Wyoming history as a teenager while interviewing pioneers for weekly vignettes published in the *Lusk Herald* in 1951. Currently, she produces an outdoor-cooking recipe column for the Wyoming State Muzzle Loading Association, coedits the Writers' Group of the Triad newsletter, and has a collection of short Wyoming historical fiction stories under way. Recently, she won her fifth award for writing. She is a part-time instructor of writing classes at Guilford Technical Community College, Jamestown, North Carolina.

She lives in Greensboro where she enjoys her "salad" garden, cat, watercolors, and friends and relatives. She loves Wyoming and North Carolina, and has a foot in both states, and wishes she could "fold the map over and step back and forth to see beloved friends and relatives on both sides."